Henry Augustin Beers

An Outline Sketch Of American Literature

Henry Augustin Beers

An Outline Sketch Of American Literature

ISBN/EAN: 9783744652179

Printed in Europe, USA, Canada, Australia, Japan

Cover: Foto ©Thomas Meinert / pixelio.de

More available books at **www.hansebooks.com**

AN

OUTLINE SKETCH

OF

AMERICAN LITERATURE.

BY

HENRY A. BEERS,

Professor of English in Yale College.

AUTHOR OF "AN OUTLINE SKETCH OF ENGLISH LITERATURE," "A CENTURY OF AMERICAN LITERATURE," "LIFE OF N. P. WILLIS," "THE THANKLESS MUSE," ETC.

NEW YORK:
CHAUTAUQUA PRESS,
C. L. S. C. Department,
805 BROADWAY.
1887.

The required books of the C. L. S. C. are recommended by a Council of six. It must, however, be understood that recommendation does not involve an approval by the Council, or by any member of it, of every principle or doctrine contained in the book recommended.

Copyright 1887, by PHILLIPS & HUNT, 805 Broadway, New York.

PREFACE.

This little volume is intended as a companion to the *Outline Sketch of English Literature*, published last year for the Chautauqua Circle. In writing it I have followed the same plan, aiming to present the subject in a sort of continuous essay rather than in the form of a "primer" or elementary manual. I have not undertaken to describe or even to mention every American author or book of importance, but only those which seemed to me of most significance. Nevertheless I believe that the sketch contains enough detail to make it of some use as a guide-book to our literature. Though meant to be mainly a history of American *belles-lettres* it makes some mention of historical and political writings, but hardly any of philosophical, scientific, and technical works.

A chronological rather than a topical order has been followed, although the fact that our best literature is of recent growth has made it impossible to adhere as closely to a chronological plan as in the English sketch. In the reading courses appended to the different chapters I have named a few of the most important authorities in American literary history, such as Duyckinck, Tyler, Stedman, and Richardson.

HENRY A. BEERS.

CONTENTS.

CHAPTER	PAGE
I. THE COLONIAL PERIOD, 1607-1765	7
II. THE REVOLUTIONARY PERIOD, 1765-1815	51
III. THE ERA OF NATIONAL EXPANSION, 1815-1837	86
IV. THE CONCORD WRITERS, 1837-1861	120
V. THE CAMBRIDGE SCHOLARS, 1837-1861	158
VI. LITERATURE IN THE CITIES, 1837-1861	197
VII. LITERATURE SINCE 1861	240
INDEX	280

OUTLINE SKETCH

OF

AMERICAN LITERATURE.

CHAPTER I.

THE COLONIAL PERIOD.

1607-1765.

THE writings of our colonial era have a much greater importance as history than as literature. It would be unfair to judge of the intellectual vigor of the English colonists in America by the books that they wrote; those "stern men with empires in their brains" had more pressing work to do than the making of books. The first settlers, indeed, were brought face to face with strange and exciting conditions—the sea, the wilderness, the Indians, the flora and fauna of a new world—things which seem stimulating to the imagination, and incidents and experiences which might have lent themselves easily to poetry or romance. Of all these they wrote back to England reports which were faithful and sometimes vivid, but which, upon the whole, hardly rise into the region of literature. "New England," said Hawthorne, "was then in a state incomparably more picturesque than at present." But to a contemporary that old New England of the seventeenth century doubtless seemed any thing but picturesque, filled with grim, hard, worky-day realities. The planters both of Virginia and Massachusetts were decimated by sickness and starvation, constantly threatened by Indian wars, and troubled by quarrels among themselves and fears of disturbance from England. The wrangles between the royal governors and the House of Burgesses in the Old Dominion, and the theological squabbles in New England, which fill our colonial records, are petty and wearisome to read of. At least, they would be so did we not bear in mind to what imperial destinies these conflicts were slowly educating the little communities which had hardly as yet secured a foothold on the edge of the raw continent.

Even a century and a half after the Jamestown and Plymouth settlements, when the American plantations had grown strong and flourishing, and commerce was building up large towns, and there were wealth and generous living and fine society, the "good old colony days when we lived under the king," had yielded little in the way of literature that is of any permanent interest. There would seem to be something in the relation of a colony to the mother country which dooms the thought and art of the former to a hopeless provincialism. Canada and Australia are great provinces, wealthier and more populous than the thirteen colonies at the time of their separation from England. They have cities whose inhabitants number hundreds of thousands, well equipped universities, libraries, cathedrals, costly public buildings, all the outward appliances of an advanced civilization; and yet what have Canada and Australia contributed to British literature?

American literature had no infancy. That engaging *naïveté* and that heroic rudeness which give a charm to the early popular tales and songs of Europe find, of course, no counterpart on our soil. Instead of emerging from the twilight of the past, the first American writings were produced under the garish noon of a modern and learned age. Decrepitude rather than youthfulness is the mark of a colonial literature. The poets, in particular, instead of finding a challenge to their imagination in the new life about them, are apt to go on imitating the cast off literary fashions of the mother country. America was settled by Englishmen who were contemporary with the greatest names in English literature. Jamestown was planted in 1607, nine years before Shakspeare's death, and the hero of that enterprize, Captain John Smith, may not improbably have been a personal acquaintance of the great dramatist. "They have acted my fatal tragedies on the stage," wrote Smith. Many circumstances in *The Tempest* were doubtless suggested by the wreck of the *Sea Venture* on "the still vext Bermoothes," as described by William Strachey in his *True Reportory of the Wrack and*

Redemption of Sir Thomas Gates, written at Jamestown, and published at London in 1510. Shakspere's contemporary, Michael Drayton, the poet of the *Polyolbion*, addressed a spirited valedictory ode to the three shiploads of "brave, heroic minds" who sailed from London in 1606 to colonize Virginia; an ode which ended with the prophecy of a future American literature:

> "And as there plenty grows
> Of laurel every-where,—
> Apollo's sacred tree—
> You it may see
> A poet's brows
> To crown, that may sing there."

Another English poet, Samuel Daniel, the author of the *Civil Wars*, had also prophesied in a similar strain:

> "And who in time knows whither we may vent
> The treasure of our tongue, to what strange shores . . .
> What worlds in the yet unformed Occident
> May come refined with accents that are ours."

It needed but a slight movement in the balances of fate, and Walter Raleigh might have been reckoned among the poets of America. He was one of the original promoters of the Virginia colony, and he made voyages in person to Newfoundland and Guiana. And more unlikely things have happened than that when John Milton left Cambridge in 1632, he should have been tempted to follow Winthrop and the colonists of Massachusetts Bay, who had sailed two years before. Sir Henry Vane, the younger, who was afterward Milton's friend—

"Vane, young in years, but in sage counsel old"—

came over in 1635, and was for a short time Governor of Massachusetts. These are idle speculations, and yet, when we reflect that Oliver Cromwell was on the point of embarking for America when he was prevented by the king's officers, we may, for the nonce, "let our frail thoughts dally with false surmise," and fancy by how narrow a chance *Paradise Lost* missed being written in Boston. But, as a rule, the members of the literary guild are not quick to emigrate. They like the feeling of an old and rich civilization about them, a state of society which America has only begun to reach during the present century.

Virginia and New England, says Lowell, were the "two great distributing centers of the English race." The men who colonized the country between the Capes of Virginia were not drawn, to any large extent, from the literary or bookish classes in the Old Country. Many of the first settlers were gentlemen—too many, Captain Smith thought, for the good of the plantation. Some among these were men of worth and spirit, "of good means and great parentage." Such was, for example, George Percy, a younger brother of the Earl of Northumberland, who was one of the original adventurers, and the author of *A Discourse of the Plantation of the Southern Colony of Virginia,* which contains a graphic narrative of the fever and famine summer of 1607 at Jamestown. But many of these gentlemen were idlers, "unruly gallants, packed thither by their friends to escape ill destinies;" dissipated younger sons, soldiers of fortune, who came over after the gold which was supposed to abound in the new country, and who spent their time in playing bowls and drinking at the tavern as soon as there was any tavern. With these was a sprinkling of mechanics and farmers, indented servants, and the off-scourings of the London streets, fruit of press gangs and jail deliveries, sent over to "work in the plantations."

Nor were the conditions of life afterward in Virginia very favorable to literary growth. The planters lived isolated on great estates, which had water fronts on the rivers that flow into the Chesapeake. There the tobacco, the chief staple of the country, was loaded directly upon the trading vessels that tied up to the long, narrow wharves of the plantations. Surrounded by his slaves, and visited occasionally by a distant neighbor, the Virginia country gentleman lived a free and careless life. He was fond of fox-hunting, horse-racing, and cock-fighting. There were no large towns, and the planters met each other mainly on occasion of a county court or the assembling of the Burgesses. The court-house was the nucleus of social and political life in Virginia as the town-meeting was in New England. In such a state of society schools were necessarily few, and popular education did not exist. Sir William Berkeley, who was the royal governor of the colony from 1641 to 1677, said, in 1670, "I thank God there are no free schools nor printing, and I hope we shall not have these hundred years." In the matter of printing, this pious wish was well-nigh realized. The first press set up in the colony, about 1681, was soon suppressed, and found no successor until the year 1729. From that date until some ten years before the Revolution one printing-press answered the needs of Virginia, and this was under official control. The earliest newspaper in the colony was the *Virginia Gazette*, established in 1736.

In the absence of schools the higher education naturally languished. Some of the planters were taught at home by tutors, and others went to England and entered the universities. But these were few in number, and there was no college in the colony until more than half a century after the foundation of Harvard in the younger province of Massachusetts. The college of William and Mary was established at Williamsburg chiefly by the exertions of the Rev. James Blair, a Scotch divine, who was sent by the Bishop of London as "commissary" to the Church in Virginia. The college received its charter in 1693, and held its first commencement in 1700. It is perhaps significant of the difference between the Puritans of New England and the so-called "Cavaliers" of Virginia, that while the former founded and supported Harvard College in 1636, and Yale in 1701, of their own motion, and at their own expense, William and Mary received its endowment from the crown, being provided for in part by a deed of lands and in part by a tax of a penny a pound on all tobacco exported from the colony. In return for this royal grant the college was to present yearly to the king two copies of Latin verse. It is reported of the young Virginian gentlemen who resorted to the new college that they brought their plantation manners with them, and were accustomed to "keep race-horses at the college, and bet at the billiard or other gaming tables." William and Mary College did a good work for the colony, and educated some of the great Virginians of the Revolutionary era, but it has never been a large or flourishing institution, and has held no such relation to the intellectual development of its section as Harvard and Yale have held in the colonies of Massachusetts and Connecticut. Even after the foundation of the University of Virginia, in which Jefferson took a conspicuous part, southern youths were commonly sent to the North for their education, and at the time of the outbreak of the civil war there was a large contingent of southern students in several northern colleges, notably in Princeton and Yale.

Naturally, the first books written in America were descriptions of the country and narratives of the vicissitudes of the infant settlements, which were sent home to be printed for the information of the English public and the encouragement of further immigration. Among books of this kind produced in Virginia the earliest and most noteworthy were the writings of that famous soldier of fortune, Captain John Smith. The first of these was his *True Relation*, namely, "of such occurrences and accidents of note as hath happened in Virginia since the first planting of that colony," printed at London in 1608. Among Smith's other books, the most important is perhaps his *General History of Virginia* (London, 1624), a compilation of various narratives by different hands, but passing under his name. Smith was a man of a restless and daring spirit, full of resource, impatient of contradiction, and of a somewhat vainglorious nature, with an appetite for the marvelous and a disposition to draw the long bow. He had seen service in many parts of the world, and his wonderful adventures lost nothing in the telling. It was alleged against him that the evidence of his prowess rested almost entirely on his own testimony. His truthfulness in essentials has not, perhaps, been successfully impugned, but his narratives have suffered by the embellishments with which he has colored them, and, in particular, the charming story of Pocohontas saving his life at the risk of her own—the one romance of early Virginian history—has passed into the realm of legend.

Captain Smith's writings have small literary value apart from the interest of the events which they describe, and the diverting but forcible personality which they unconsciously display. They are the rough-hewn records of a busy man of action, whose sword was mightier than his pen. As Smith returned to England after two years in Virginia, and did not permanently cast in his lot with the settlement of which he had been for a time the leading spirit, he can hardly be claimed as an American author. No more can Mr. George Sandys, who came to Virginia in the train of Governor Wyat, in 1621, and completed his excellent metrical translation of Ovid on the banks of the James, in the midst of the Indian massacre of 1622, "limned" as he writes "by that imperfect light which was snatched from the hours of night and repose, having wars and tumults to bring it to light instead of the muses." Sandys went back to England for good, probably as early as 1625, and can, therefore, no more be reckoned as the first American poet, on the strength of his paraphrase of the *Metamorphoses*, than he can be reckoned the earliest Yankee inventor, because he "introduced the first water-mill into America."

The literature of colonial Virginia, and of the southern colonies which took their point of departure from Virginia, is almost wholly of this historical and descriptive kind. A great part of it is concerned with the internal affairs of the province, such as "Bacon's Rebellion," in 1676, one of the most striking episodes in our ante-revolutionary annals, and of which there exist a number of narratives, some of them anonymous, and only rescued from a manuscript condition a hundred years after the event. Another part is concerned with the explorations of new territory. Such were the "Westover Manuscripts," left by Colonel William Byrd, who was appointed in 1729 one of the commissioners to fix the boundary between Virginia and North Carolina, and gave an account of the survey in his *History of the Dividing Line*, which was only printed in 1841. Colonel Byrd is one of the most brilliant figures of colonial Virginia, and a type of the Old Virginia gentleman. He had been sent to England for his education, where he was admitted to the bar of the Middle Temple, elected a Fellow of the Royal Society, and formed an intimate friendship with Charles Boyle, the Earl of Orrery. He held many offices in the government of the colony, and founded the cities of Richmond and Petersburg. His estates were large, and at Westover—where he had one of the finest private libraries in America—he exercised a baronial hospitality, blending the usual profusion of plantation life with the elegance of a traveled scholar and "picked man of countries." Colonel Byrd was rather an amateur in literature. His *History of the Dividing Line* is written with a jocularity which rises occasionally into real humor, and which gives to the painful journey through the wilderness the air of a holiday expedition. Similar in tone were his diaries of *A Progress to the Mines* and *A Journey to the Land of Eden* in North Carolina.

The first formal historian of Virginia was Robert Berkeley, "a native and inhabitant of the place," whose *History of Virginia* was printed at London in 1705. Beverley was a rich planter and large slave owner, who, being in London in 1703, was shown by his bookseller the manuscript of a forthcoming work, Oldmixon's *British Empire in America*. Beverley was set upon writing his history by the inaccuracies in this, and likewise because the province "has been so misrepresented to the common people of England as to make them believe that the servants in Virginia are made to draw in cart and plow, and that the country turns all people black," an impression which lingers still in parts of Europe. The most original portions of the book are those in which the author puts down his personal observations of the plants and animals of the New World, and particularly the account of the Indians, to which his third book is devoted, and which is accompanied by valuable plates. Beverley's knowledge of these matters was evidently at first hand, and his descriptions here are very fresh and interesting. The more strictly historical part of his work is not free from prejudice and inaccuracy. A more critical, detailed, and impartial, but much less readable, work was William Stith's *History of the First Discovery and Settlement of Virginia*, 1747, which brought the subject down only to the year 1624. Stith was a clergyman, and at one time a professor in William and Mary College.

The Virginians were stanch royalists and churchmen. The Church of England was established by law, and non-conformity was persecuted in various ways. Three missionaries were sent to the colony in 1642 by the Puritans of New England, two from Braintree, Massachusetts, and one from New Haven. They were not suffered to preach, but many resorted to them in private houses, until, being finally driven out by fines and imprisonments, they took refuge in Catholic Maryland. The Virginia clergy were not, as a body, very much of a force in education or literature. Many of them, by reason of the scattering and dispersed condition of their parishes, lived as domestic chaplains with the wealthier planters, and partook of their illiteracy and their passion for gaming and hunting. Few of them inherited the zeal of Alexander Whitaker, the "Apostle of Virginia," who came over in 1611 to preach to the colonists and convert the Indians, and who published in furtherance of those ends *Good News from Virginia*, in 1613, three years before his death by drowning in James River.

The conditions were much more favorable for the production of a literature in New England than in the southern colonies. The free and genial existence of the "Old Dominion" had no counterpart among the settlers of Plymouth and Massachusetts Bay, and the Puritans must have been rather unpleasant people to live with for persons of a different way of thinking. But their intensity of character, their respect for learning, and the heroic mood which sustained them through the hardships and dangers of their great enterprise are amply reflected in their own writings. If these are not so much literature as the raw materials of literature, they have at least been fortunate in finding interpreters among their descendants, and no modern Virginian has done for the memory of the Jamestown planters what Hawthorne, Whittier, Longfellow, and others have done in casting the glamour of poetry and romance over the lives of the founders of New England.

Cotton Mather, in his *Magnalia*, quotes the following passage from one of those election sermons, delivered before the General Court of Massachusetts, which formed for many years the great annual intellectual event of the colony: " The question was often put unto our predecessors, *What went ye out into the wilderness to see?* And the answer to it is not only too excellent but too notorious to be dissembled. . . . We came hither because we would have our posterity settled under the pure and full dispensations of the gospel, defended by rulers that should be of ourselves." The New England colonies were, in fact, theocracies. Their leaders were clergymen or laymen, whose zeal for the faith was no whit inferior to that of the ministers themselves. Church and State were one. The freeman's oath was only administered to Church members, and there was no place in the social system for unbelievers or dissenters. The Pilgrim fathers regarded their transplantation to the New World as an exile, and nothing is more touching in their written records than the repeated expressions of love and longing toward the old home which they had left, and even toward that Church of England from which they had sorrowfully separated themselves. It was not in any light or adventurous spirit that they faced the perils of the sea and the wilderness. "This howling wilderness," "these ends of the earth," " these goings down of the sun," are some of the epithets which they constantly applied to the land of their exile. Nevertheless they had come to stay, and, unlike Smith and Percy and Sandys, the early historians and writers of New England cast in their lots permanently with the new settlements. A few, indeed, went back after 1640—Mather says some ten or twelve of the ministers of the first "classis" or immigration were among them—when the victory of the Puritanic party in Parliament opened a career for them in England, and made their presence there seem in some cases a duty. The celebrated Hugh Peters, for example, who was afterward Oliver Cromwell's chaplain, and was beheaded after the Restoration, went back in 1641, and in 1647 Nathaniel Ward, the minister of Ipswich, Massachusetts, and author of a quaint book against toleration, entitled *The Simple Cobbler of Agawam*, written in America and published shortly after its author's arrival in England. The Civil War, too, put a stop to further emigration from England until after the Restoration in 1660.

The mass of the Puritan immigration consisted of men of the middle class, artisans and husbandmen, the most useful members of a new colony. But their leaders were clergymen educated at the universities, and especially at Emanuel College, Cambridge, the great Puritan college; their civil magistrates were also in great part gentlemen of education and substance, like the elder Winthrop, who was learned in the law, and Theophilus Eaton, first governor of New Haven, who was a London merchant of good estate. It is computed that there were in New England during the first generation as many university graduates as in any community of equal population in the old country. Almost the first care of the settlers was to establish schools. Every town of fifty families was required by law to maintain a common school, and every town of a hundred families a grammar or Latin school. In 1636, only sixteen years after the landing of the Pilgrims on Plymouth Rock, Harvard College was founded at Newtown, whose name was thereupon changed to Cambridge, the General Court held at Boston on September 8, 1680, having already advanced £400 "by way of essay towards the building of something to begin a college." "An university," says Mather, "which hath been to these plantations, for the good literature there cultivated, *sal Gentium* . . . and a river, without the streams whereof these regions would have been mere unwatered places for the devil." By 1701 Harvard had put forth a vigorous offshoot, Yale College, at New Haven, the settlers of New Haven and Connecticut plantations having increased sufficiently to need a college at their own doors. A printing press was set up at Cambridge in 1639, which was under the oversight of the university authorities, and afterwards of licensers appointed by the civil power. The press was no more free in Massachusetts than in Virginia, and that "liberty of unlicensed printing," for which the Puritan Milton had pleaded in his *Areopagitica*, in 1644, was unknown in Puritan New England until some twenty years before the outbreak of the Revolutionary War. "The Freeman's Oath" and an almanac were issued from the Cambridge press in 1639, and in 1640 the first English book printed in America, a collection of the psalms in meter, made by various ministers, and known as the *Bay Psalm Book*. The poetry of this version was worse, if possible, than that of Sternhold and Hopkins's famous rendering; but it is noteworthy that one of the principal translators was that devoted "Apostle to the Indians," the Rev. John Eliot, who, in 1661–63, translated the Bible into the Algonkin tongue. Eliot hoped and toiled a lifetime for the conversion of those "salvages," "tawnies," "devil-worshipers," for whom our early writers have usually nothing but bad words. They have been destroyed instead of converted; but his (so entitled) *Mamusse Wunnectupanatamwe Up-*

Biblum God naneeswe Nukkone Testament kah wonk Wusku Testament—the first Bible printed in America—remains a monument of missionary zeal and a work of great value to students of the Indian languages.

A modern writer has said that, to one looking back on the history of old New England, it seems as though the sun shone but dimly there, and the landscape was always dark and wintry. Such is the impression which one carries away from the perusal of books like Bradford's and Winthrop's *Journals*, or Mather's *Wonders of the Invisible World:* an impression of gloom, of night and cold, of mysterious fears besieging the infant settlements, scattered in a narrow fringe "between the groaning forest and the shore." The Indian terror hung over New England for more than half a century, or until the issue of King Philip's War, in 1676, relieved the colonists of any danger of a general massacre. Added to this were the perplexities caused by the earnest resolve of the settlers to keep their New English Eden free from the intrusion of the serpent in the shape of heretical sects in religion. The Puritanism of Massachusetts was an orthodox and conservative Puritanism. The later and more grotesque out-crops of the movement in the old England found no toleration in the new. But these refugees for conscience' sake were compelled in turn to persecute Antinomians, Separatists, Familists, Libertines, Anti-pedobaptists, and later, Quakers, and still later, Enthusiasts, who swarmed into their precincts and troubled the Churches with "prophesyings" and novel opinions. Some of these were banished, others were flogged or imprisoned, and a few were put to death. Of the exiles the most noteworthy was Roger Williams, an impetuous, warm-hearted man, who was so far in advance of his age as to deny the power of the civil magistrate in cases of conscience, or who, in other words, maintained the modern doctrine of the separation of Church and State. Williams was driven away from the Massachusetts colony — where he had been minister of the Church at Salem—and with a few followers fled into the southern wilderness, and settled at Providence. There and in the neighboring plantation of Rhode Island, for which he obtained a charter, he established his patriarchal rule, and gave freedom of worship to all comers. Williams was a prolific writer on theological subjects, the most important of his writings being, perhaps, his *Bloody Tenent of Persecution*, 1644, and a supplement to the same called out by a reply to the former work from the pen of Mr. John Cotton, minister of the First Church at Boston, entitled *The Bloody Tenent Washed and made White in the Blood of the Lamb*. Williams was also a friend to the Indians, whose lands, he thought, should not be taken from them without payment, and he anticipated Eliot by writing, in 1643, a *Key into the Language of America*. Although at odds with the theology of Massachusetts Bay, Williams remained in correspondence with Winthrop and others in Boston, by whom he was highly esteemed. He visited England in 1643 and 1652, and made the acquaintance of John Milton.

Besides the threat of an Indian war and their anxious concern for the purity of the Gospel in their Churches, the colonists were haunted by superstitious forebodings of the darkest kind. It seemed to them that Satan, angered by the setting up of the kingdom of the saints in America, had "come down in great wrath," and was present among them, sometimes even in visible shape, to terrify and tempt. Special providences and unusual phenomena, like earthquakes, mirages, and the northern lights, are gravely recorded by Winthrop and Mather and others as portents of supernatural persecutions. Thus Mrs. Anne Hutchinson, the celebrated leader of the Familists, having, according to rumor, been delivered of a monstrous birth, the Rev. John Cotton, in open assembly, at Boston, upon a lecture day, "thereupon gathered that it might signify her error in denying inherent righteousness." "There will be an unusual range of the devil among us," wrote Mather, "a little before the second coming of our Lord. The evening wolves will be much abroad when we are near the evening of the world." This belief culminated in the horrible witchcraft delusion at Salem in 1692, that "spectral puppet play," which, beginning with the malicious pranks of a few children who accused certain uncanny old women and other persons of mean condition and suspected lives of having tormented them with magic, gradually drew into its vortex victims of the highest character, and resulted in the judicial murder of over nineteen people. Many of the possessed pretended to have been visited by the apparition of a little black man, who urged them to inscribe their names in a red book which he carried—a sort of muster-roll of those who had forsworn God's service for the devil's. Others testified to having been present at meetings of witches in the forest. It is difficult now to read without contempt the "evidence" which grave justices and learned divines considered sufficient to condemn to death men and women of unblemished lives. It is true that the belief in witchcraft was general at that time all over the civilized world, and that sporadic cases of witch-burnings had occurred in different parts of America and Europe. Sir Thomas Browne, in his *Religio Medici*, 1635, affirmed his belief in witches, and pronounced those who doubted of them " a sort of atheist." But the superstition came to a head in the Salem trials and executions, and was the more shocking from the general high level of intelligence in the community in which these were held. It would be well if those who lament the decay of "faith" would remember what things were done in New England in the name of faith less than two hundred years ago. It is not wonderful that, to the Massachusetts Puritans of the seventeenth century, the mysterious forest held no beautiful suggestion; to them it was simply a grim and hideous wilderness, whose dark aisles were the ambush of prowling savages and the rendezvous of those other "devil-worshipers" who celebrated there a kind of vulgar Walpurgis night.

The most important of original sources for the history of the settlement of New England are the journals of William Bradford, first governor of Plymouth, and John Winthrop, the second governor of Massachusetts, which hold a place corresponding to the writings of Captain John Smith in the Virginia colony, but are much more sober and trustworthy. Bradford's *History of Plymouth Plantation* covers the period from 1620 to 1646. The manuscript was used by later annalists, but remained unpublished, as a whole, until 1855, having been lost during the war of the revolution and recovered long afterward in England. Winthrop's Journal, or *History of New England*, begun on shipboard in 1630, and extending to 1649, was not published entire until 1826. It is of equal authority with Bradford's, and perhaps, on the whole, the more important of the two, as the colony of Massachusetts Bay, whose history it narrates, greatly outwent Plymouth in wealth and population, though not in priority of settlement. The interest of Winthrop's Journal lies in the events that it records rather than in any charm in the historian's manner of recording them. His style is pragmatic, and some of the incidents which he gravely notes are trivial to the modern mind, though instructive as to our forefathers' way of thinking. For instance, of the year 1632: "At Watertown there was (in the view of divers witnesses) a great combat between a mouse and a snake, and after a long fight the mouse prevailed and killed the snake. The pastor of Boston, Mr. Wilson, a very sincere, holy man, hearing of it, gave this interpretation: that the snake was the devil, the mouse was a poor, contemptible people, which God had brought hither, which should overcome Satan here and dispossess him of his kingdom." The reader of Winthrop's *Journal* comes every-where upon hints which the imagination has since shaped into poetry and romance. The germs of many of Longfellow's *New England Tragedies*, of Hawthorne's *Maypole of Merrymount*, of Endicott's *Red Cross*, and of Whittier's *John Underhill* and *The Familists' Hymn* are all to be found in some dry, brief entry of the old Puritan diarist. "Robert Cole, having been oft punished for drunkenness, was now ordered to wear a red D about his neck for a year," to wit, the year 1633, and thereby gave occasion to the greatest American romance, *The Scarlet Letter*. The famous apparition of the phantom ship in New Haven harbor, "upon the top of the poop a man standing with one hand akimbo under his left side, and in his right hand a sword stretched out toward the sea," was first chronicled by Winthrop under the year 1648. This meterological phenomenon took on the dimensions of a full-grown myth some forty years later, as related, with many embellishments, by Rev. James Pierpont, of New Haven, in a letter to Cotton Mather. Winthrop put great faith in special providences, and among other instances narrates, not without a certain grim satisfaction, how "the *Mary Rose*, a ship of Bristol, of about 200 tons," lying before Charleston, was blown in pieces with her own powder, being twenty-one barrels, wherein the judgment of God appeared, "for the master and company were many of them profane scoffers at us and at the ordinances of religion here." Without any effort at dramatic portraiture or character sketching, Winthrop managed in all simplicity, and by the plain relation of facts, to leave a clear impression of many of the prominent figures in the first Massachusetts immigration. In particular there gradually arises from the entries in his diary a very distinct and diverting outline of Captain John Underhill, celebrated in Whittier's poem. He was one of the few professional soldiers who came over with the Puritan fathers, such as John Mason, the hero of the Pequot War, and Miles Standish, whose *Courtship* Longfellow sang. He had seen service in the Low Countries, and in pleading the privilege of his profession "he insisted much upon the liberty which all States do allow to military officers for free speech, etc., and that himself had spoken sometimes as freely to Count Nassau." Captain Underhill gave the colony no end of trouble, both by his scandalous living and his heresies in religion. Having been seduced into Familistical opinions by Mrs. Anne Hutchinson, who was banished for her beliefs, he was had up before the General Court and questioned, among other points, as to his own report of the manner of his conversion. "He had lain under a spirit of bondage and a legal way for years, and could get no assurance, till, at length, as he was taking a pipe of tobacco, the Spirit set home an absolute promise of free grace with such assurance and joy as he never since doubted of his good estate, neither should he, though he should fall into sin. . . . The Lord's day following he made a speech in the assembly, showing that as the Lord was pleased to convert Paul as he was in persecuting, etc., so he might manifest himself to him as he was taking the moderate use of the creature called tobacco." The gallant captain, being banished the colony, betook himself to the falls of the Piscataquack (Exeter, N. H.), where the Rev. John Wheelwright, another adherent of Mrs. Hutchinson, had gathered a congregation. Being made governor of this plantation, Underhill sent letters to the Massachusetts magistrates, breathing reproaches and imprecations of vengeance. But meanwhile it was discovered that he had been living in adultery at Boston with a young woman whom he had seduced, the wife of a cooper, and the captain was forced to make public confession, which he did with great unction and in a manner highly dramatic. "He came in his worst clothes (being accustomed to take great pride in his bravery and neatness), without a band, in a foul linen cap, and pulled close to his eyes, and standing upon a form, he did, with many deep sighs and abundance of tears, lay open his wicked course." There is a lurking humor in the grave Winthrop's detailed account of Underhill's doings. Winthrop's own personality comes out well in his *Journal*. He was a born leader of men, a *conditor imperii*, just, moderate, patient, wise, and his narrative gives, upon the whole, a favorable impression of the general prudence and fair-mindedness of the Massachusetts settlers in their dealings with one another, with the Indians, and with the neighboring plantations.

Considering our forefathers' errand and calling into this wilderness, it is not strange that their chief literary staples were sermons and tracts in controversial theology. Multitudes of these were written and published by the divines of the first generation, such as John Cotton, Thomas Shepard, John Norton, Peter Bulkley, and Thomas Hooker, the founder of Hartford, of whom it was finely said that "when he was doing his Master's business he would put a king into his pocket." Nor were their successors in the second or the third generation any less industrious and prolific. They rest from their labors and their works do follow them. Their sermons and theological treatises are not literature, they are for the most part dry, heavy, and dogmatic, but they exhibit great learning, logical acuteness, and an earnestness which sometimes rises into eloquence. The pulpit ruled New England, and the sermon was the great intellectual engine of the time. The serious thinking of the Puritans was given almost exclusively to religion; the other world was all their art. The daily secular events of life, the aspects of nature, the vicissitude of the seasons, were important enough to find record in print only in so far as they manifested God's dealings with his people. So much was the sermon depended upon to furnish literary food that it was the general custom of serious minded laymen to take down the words of the discourse in their note-books. Franklin, in his *Autobiography*, describes this as the constant habit of his grandfather, Peter Folger; and Mather, in his life of the elder Winthrop, says that "tho' he wrote not after the preacher, yet such was his *attention* and such his *retention* in hearing, that he repeated unto his family the sermons which he had heard in the congregation." These discourses were commonly of great length; twice, or sometimes thrice, the pulpit hour-glass was silently inverted while the orator pursued his theme even unto n'thly.

The book which best sums up the life and thought of this old New England of the seventeenth century is Cotton Mather's *Magnalia Christi Americana*. Mather was by birth a member of that clerical aristocracy which developed later into Dr. Holmes's "Brahmin Caste of New England." His maternal grandfather was John Cotton. His father was Increase Mather, the most learned divine of his generation in New England, minister of the North Church of Boston, President of Harvard College, and author, *inter alia*, of that characteristically Puritan book, *An Essay for the Recording of Illustrious Providences.* Cotton Mather himself was a monster of erudition and a prodigy of diligence. He was graduated from Harvard at fifteen. He ordered his daily life and conversation by a system of minute observances. He was a book-worm, whose life was spent between his library and his pulpit, and his published works number upward of three hundred and eighty. Of these the most important is the *Magnalia*, 1702, an ecclesiastical history of New England from 1620 to 1698, divided into seven parts: I. Antiquities; II. Lives of the Governors; III. Lives of Sixty Famous Divines; IV. A History of Harvard College, with biographies of its eminent graduates; V. Acts and Monuments of the Faith; VI. Wonderful Providences; VII. The Wars of the Lord, that is, an account of the Afflictions and Disturbances of the Churches and the Conflicts with the Indians. The plan of the work thus united that of Fuller's *Worthies of England* and *Church History* with that of Wood's *Athenæ Oxonienses* and Fox's *Book of Martyrs.*

Mather's prose was of the kind which the English Commonwealth writers used. He was younger by a generation than Dryden; but as literary fashions are slower to change in a colony than in the mother country, that nimble English which Dryden and the Restoration essayists introduced had not yet displaced in New England the older manner. Mather wrote in the full and pregnant style of Taylor, Milton, Brown, Fuller, and Burton, a style ponderous with learning and stiff with allusions, digressions, conceits, anecdotes, and quotations from the Greek and the Latin. A page of the *Magnalia* is almost as richly mottled with italics as one from the *Anatomy of Melancholy*, and the quaintness which Mather caught from his favorite Fuller disports itself in textual pun and marginal anagram and the fantastic sub-titles of his books and chapters. He speaks of Thomas Hooker as having "*angled* many scores of souls into the kingdom of heaven," anagrammatizes Mrs. Hutchinson's surname into "the non-such;" and having occasion to speak of Mr. Urian Oaks's election to the presidency of Harvard College, enlarges upon the circumstance as follows:

"We all know that *Britain* knew nothing more famous than their ancient sect of DRUIDS; the philosophers, whose order, they say, was instituted by one *Samothes*, which is in English as much as to say, *an heavenly man*. The *Celtic* name *Deru*, for an *Oak* was that from whence they received their denomination; as at this very day the *Welch* call this tree *Drew*, and this order of men *Derwyddon*. But there are no small antiquaries who derive this *oaken religion* and *philosophy* from the *Oaks of Mamre*, where the Patriarch *Abraham* had as well a dwelling as an *altar*. That *Oaken-Plain* and the eminent OAK under which *Abraham* lodged was extant in the days of *Constantine*, as *Isidore*, *Jerom*, and *Sozomen* have assured us. Yea, there are shrewd probabilities that *Noah* himself had lived in this very *Oak-plain* before him; for this very place was called Ογγη, which was the name of *Noah*, so styled from the *Oggyan* (*subcineritiis panibus*) sacrifices, which he did use to offer in this renowned *Grove*. And it was from this example that the ancients and particularly that the Druids of the nations, chose *oaken* retirements for their studies. Reader, let us now, upon another account, behold the students of *Harvard College*, as a rendezvous of happy *Druids*, under the influences of so rare a president. But, alas! our joy must be short-lived, for on *July* 25, 1681, the stroke of a sudden death felled the *tree*,

"Qui tantum inter caput extulit omnes
Quantum lenta solent inter viberna cypressi.

Mr. *Oakes* thus being transplanted into the better world, the presidentship was immediately tendered unto *Mr. Increase Mather*."

This will suffice as an example of the bad taste and laborious pedantry which disfigured Mather's writing. In its substance the book is a perfect thesaurus; and inasmuch as nothing is unimportant in the history of the beginnings of such a nation as this is and is destined to be, the *Magnalia* will always remain a valuable and interesting work.

Cotton Mather, born in 1663, was of the second generation of Americans, his grandfather being of the immigration, but his father a native of Dorchester, Mass. A comparison of his writings and of the writings of his contemporaries with the works of Bradford, Winthrop, Hooker, and others of the original colonists, shows that the simple and heroic faith of the Pilgrims had hardened into formalism and doctrinal rigidity. The leaders of the Puritan exodus, notwithstanding their intolerance of errors in belief, were comparatively broad-minded men. They were sharers in a great national movement, and they came over when their cause was warm with the glow of martyrdom and on the eve of its coming triumph at home. After the Restoration, in 1660, the currents of national feeling no longer circulated so freely through this distant member of the body politic, and thought in America became more provincial. The English dissenters, though socially at a disadvantage as compared with the Church of England, had the great benefit of living at the center of national life, and of feeling about them the pressure of vast bodies of people who did not think as they did. In New England, for many generations, the dominant sect had things all its own way, a condition of things which is not healthy for any sect or party. Hence Mather and the divines of his time appear in their writings very much like so many Puritan bishops, jealous of their prerogatives, magnifying their apostolate, and careful to maintain their authority over the laity. Mather had an appetite for the marvelous, and took a leading part in the witchcraft trials, of which he gave an account in his *Wonders of the Invisible World*, 1693. To the quaint pages of the *Magnalia* our modern authors have resorted as to a collection of romances or fairy tales. Whittier, for example, took from thence the subject of his poem *The Garrison of Cape Anne;* and Hawthorne embodied in *Grandfather's Chair* the most elaborate of Mather's biographies. This was the life of Sir William Phipps, who, from being a poor shepherd boy in his native province of Maine, rose to be the royal governor of Massachusetts, and the story of whose wonderful adventures in raising the freight of a Spanish treasure ship, sunk on a reef near Port de la Plata, reads less like sober fact than like some ancient fable, with talk of the Spanish main, bullion, and plate and jewels and "pieces of eight."

Of Mather's generation was Samuel Sewall, Chief Justice of Massachusetts, a singularly gracious and venerable figure, who is intimately known through his *Diary* kept from 1673 to 1729. This has been compared with the more famous diary of Samuel Pepys, which it resembles in its confidential character and the completeness of its self-revelation, but to which it is as much inferior in historic interest as "the petty province here" was inferior in political and social importance to "Britain far away." For the most part it is a chronicle of small beer, the diarist jotting down the minutiæ of his domestic life and private affairs, even to the recording of such haps as this: " March 23, I had my hair cut by G. Barret." But it also affords instructive glimpses of public events, such as King Philip's War, the Quaker troubles, the English Revolution of 1688, etc. It bears about the same relation to New England history at the close of the seventeenth century as Bradford's and Winthrop's journals bear to that of the first generation. Sewall was one of the justices who presided at the trial of the Salem witches; but for the part which he took in that wretched affair he made such atonement as was possible, by open confession of his mistake and his remorse in the presence of the Church. Sewall was one of the first writers against African slavery, in his brief tract, *The Selling of Joseph*, printed at Boston in 1700. His *Phenomena Quædam Apocalyptica*, a mystical interpretation of prophecies concerning the New Jerusalem, which he identifies with America, is remembered only because Whittier, in his *Prophecy of Samuel Sewall*, has paraphrased one poetic passage, which shows a loving observation of nature very rare in our colonial writers.

Of poetry, indeed, or, in fact, of pure literature, in the narrower sense—that is, of the imaginative representation of life—there was little or none in the colonial period. There were no novels, no plays, no satires, and—until the example of the *Spectator* had begun to work on this side the water—no experiments even at the lighter forms of essay writing, character sketches, and literary criticism. There was verse of a certain kind, but the most generous stretch of the term would hardly allow it to be called poetry. Many of the early divines of New England relieved their pens, in the intervals of sermon writing, of epigrams, elegies, eulogistic verses, and similar grave trifles distinguished by the crabbed wit of the so-called "metaphysical poets," whose manner was in fashion when the Puritans left England; the manner of Donne and Cowley, and those darlings of the New English muse, the *Emblems* of Quarles and the *Divine Week* of Du Bartas, as translated by Sylvester. The *Magnalia* contains a number of these things in Latin and English, and is itself well bolstered with complimentary introductions in meter by the author's friends. For example:

COTTONIUS MATHERUS.

ANAGRAM.

Tuos Tecum Ornasti.

"While thus the dead in thy rare pages rise
Thine, with thyself, thou dost immortalize.
To view the odds thy learned lives invite
'Twixt Eleutherian and Edomite.
But all succeeding ages shall despair
A fitting monument for thee to *rear.*
Thy own rich pen (peace, silly Momus, peace!)
Hath given them a lasting *writ of ease.*"

The epitaphs and mortuary verses were especially ingenious in the matter of puns, anagrams, and similar conceits. The death of the Rev. Samuel Stone, of Hartford, afforded an opportunity of this sort not to be missed, and his threnodist accordingly celebrated him as a "whetstone," a "loadstone," an "Ebenezer"—

> "A stone for kingly David's use so fit
> As would not fail Goliah's front to hit," etc.

The most characteristic, popular, and widely circulated poem of colonial New England was Michael Wigglesworth's *Day of Doom* (1662), a kind of doggerel *Inferno*, which went through nine editions, and "was the solace," says Lowell, "of every fireside; the flicker of the pine-knots by which it was conned perhaps adding a livelier relish to its premonitions of eternal combustion." Wigglesworth had not the technical equipment of a poet. His verse is sing-song, his language rude and monotonous, and the lurid horrors of his material hell are more likely to move mirth than fear in a modern reader. But there are an unmistakable vigor of imagination and a sincerity of belief in his gloomy poem which hold it far above contempt, and easily account for its universal currency among a people like the Puritans. One stanza has been often quoted for its grim concession to unregenerate infants of "the easiest room in hell"—a *limbus infantum* which even Origen need not have scrupled at.

The most authoritative expounder of New England Calvinism was Jonathan Edwards (1703-

1758), a native of Connecticut, and a graduate of Yale, who was minister for more than twenty years over the Church in Northampton, Mass., afterward missionary to the Stockbridge Indians, and at the time of his death had just been inaugurated president of Princeton College. By virtue of his *Inquiry into the Freedom of the Will*, 1754, Edwards holds rank as the subtlest metaphysician of his age. This treatise was composed to justify, on philosophical grounds, the Calvinistic doctrines of foreordination and election by grace, though its arguments are curiously coincident with those of the scientific necessitarians, whose conclusions are as far asunder from Edwards's "as from the center thrice to the utmost pole." His writings belong to theology rather than to literature, but there is an intensity and a spiritual elevation about them, apart from the profundity and acuteness of the thought, which lift them here and there into the finer ether of purely emotional or imaginative art. He dwelt rather upon the terrors than the comfort of the word, and his chosen themes were the dogmas of predestination, original sin, total depravity, and eternal punishment. The titles of his sermons are significant: *Men Naturally God's Enemies, Wrath upon the Wicked to the Uttermost, The Final Judgment*, etc. "A natural man," he wrote in the first of these discourses, "has a heart like the heart of a devil. . . . The heart of a natural man is as destitute of love to God as a dead, stiff, cold corpse is of vital heat." Perhaps the most famous of Edwards's sermons was *Sinners in the Hands of an Angry God*, preached at Enfield, Conn., July 8, 1741, "at a time of great awakenings," and upon the ominous text, *Their foot shall slide in due time*. "The God that holds you over the pit of hell" runs an oft-quoted passage from this powerful denunciation of the wrath to come, "much as one holds a spider or some loathsome insect over the fire, abhors you, and is dreadfully provoked. . . . You are ten thousand times more abominable in his eyes than the most hateful venomous serpent is in ours. . . . You hang by a slender thread, with the flames of divine wrath flashing about it. . . . If you cry to God to pity you, he will be so far from pitying you in your doleful case that he will only tread you under foot. . . . He will crush out your blood and make it fly, and it shall be sprinkled on his garments so as to stain all his raiment." But Edwards was a rapt soul, possessed with the love as well as the fear of the God, and there are passages of sweet and exalted feeling in his *Treatise Concerning Religious Affections*, 1746. Such is his portrait of Sarah Pierpont, "a young lady in New Haven," who afterward became his wife, and who "will sometimes go about from place to place singing sweetly, and no one knows for what. She loves to be alone, walking in the fields and groves, and seems to have some one invisible always conversing with her." Edwards's printed works number thirty-six titles. A complete edition of them in ten volumes was published in 1829 by his great-grandson, Sereno Dwight. The memoranda from Edwards's note-books, quoted by his editor and biographer, exhibit a remarkable precocity. Even as a school-boy and a college student he had made deep guesses in physics as well as metaphysics, and, as might have been predicted of a youth of his philosophical insight and ideal cast of mind, he had early anticipated Berkeley in denying the existence of matter. In passing from Mather to Edwards, we step from the seventeenth to the eighteenth century. There is the same difference between them in style and turn of thought as between Milton and Locke, or between Fuller and Dryden. The learned digressions, the witty conceits, the perpetual interlarding of the text with scraps of Latin, have fallen off, even as the full-bottomed wig and the clerical gown and bands have been laid aside for the undistinguishing dress of the modern minister. In Edwards's English all is simple, precise, direct, and business-like.

Benjamin Franklin (1706–1790), who was strictly contemporary with Edwards, was a contrast to him in every respect. As Edwards represents the spirituality and other-worldliness of Puritanism, Franklin stands for the worldly and secular side of American character, and he illustrates the development of the New England Englishman into the modern Yankee. Clear rather than subtle, without ideality or romance or fineness of emotion or poetic lift, intensely practical and utilitarian, broad-minded, inventive, shrewd, versatile, Franklin's sturdy figure became typical of his time and his people. He was the first and the only man of letters in colonial America who acquired a cosmopolitan fame, and impressed his characteristic Americanism upon the mind of Europe. He was the embodiment of common sense and of the useful virtues; with the enterprise but without the nervousness of his modern compatriots, uniting the philosopher's openness of mind with the sagacity and quickness of resource of the self-made business man. He was representative also of his age, an age of *aufklärung*, *eclaircissement*, or "clearing up." By the middle of the eighteenth century a change had taken place in American society. Trade had increased between the different colonies; Boston, New York, and Philadelphia were considerable towns; democratic feeling was spreading; over forty newspapers were published in America at the outbreak of the Revolution; politics claimed more attention than formerly, and theology less. With all this intercourse and mutual reaction of the various colonies upon one another, the isolated theocracy of New England naturally relaxed somewhat of its grip on the minds of the laity. When Franklin was a printer's apprentice in Boston, setting type on his brother's *New England Courant*, the fourth American newspaper, he got hold of an odd volume of the *Spectator*, and formed his style upon Addison, whose manner he afterward imitated in his *Busy-Body* papers in the Philadelphia *Weekly Mercury*. He also read Locke and the English deistical writers, Collins and Shaftesbury, and became himself a deist and free-thinker; and subsequently when practicing his trade in London, in 1724-26, he made the acquaintance of Dr. Mandeville, author of the *Fable of the Bees*, at a pale-ale house in Cheapside, called "The Horns," where the famous free-thinker presided over a club of wits and boon companions. Though a native of Boston, Franklin is identified with Philadelphia, whither he arrived in 1723, a runaway 'prentice boy, "whose stock of cash consisted of a Dutch dollar and about a shilling in copper." The description in his *Autobiography* of his walking up Market Street munching a loaf of bread, and passing his future wife, standing on her father's doorstep, has become almost as familiar as the anecdote about Whittington and his cat.

It was in the practical sphere that Franklin was greatest, as an originator and executor of projects for the general welfare. The list of his public services is almost endless. He organized the Philadelphia fire department and street cleaning service, and the colonial postal system which grew into the United States Post Office Department. He started the Philadelphia public library, the American Philosophical Society, the University of Pennsylvania, and the first American magazine, *The General Magazine and Historical Chronicle;* so that he was almost singly the father of whatever intellectual life the Pennsylvania colony could boast of. In 1754, when commissioners from the colonies met at Albany, Franklin proposed a plan, which was adopted, for the union of all the colonies under one government. But all these things, as well as his mission to England in 1757, on behalf of the Pennsylvania Assembly in its dispute with the proprietaries; his share in the Declaration of Independence—of which he was one of the signers—and his residence in France as Embassador of the United Colonies, belong to the political history of the country; to the history of American science belong his celebrated experiments in electricity; and his benefits to mankind in both of these departments were aptly summed up in the famous epigram of the French statesman Turgot:

"*Erupuit coelo fulmen sceptrumque tyrannis.*"

Franklin's success in Europe was such as no American had yet achieved, as few Americans since him have achieved. Hume and Voltaire were among his acquaintances and his professed admirers. In France he was fairly idolized, and when he died Mirabeau announced, "The genius which has freed America and poured a flood of light over Europe has returned to the bosom of the Divinity."

Franklin was a great man, but hardly a great writer, though as a writer, too, he had many admirable and some great qualities. Among these were the crystal clearness and simplicity of his style. His more strictly literary performances, such as his essays after the *Spectator*, hardly rise above mediocrity, and are neither better nor worse than other imitations of Addison. But in some of his lighter bagatelles there are a homely wisdom and a charming playfulness which have won them enduring favor. Such are his famous story of the *Whistle*, his *Dialogue between Franklin and the Gout*, his letters to Madame Helvetius, and his verses entitled *Paper*. The greater portion of his writings consists of papers on general politics, commerce, and political economy, contributions to the public questions of his day. These are of the nature of journalism rather than of literature, and many of them were published in his newspaper, the *Pennsylvania Gazette*, the medium through which for many years he most strongly influenced American opinion. The most popular of his writings were his *Autobiography* and *Poor Richard's Almanac*. The former of these was begun in 1771, resumed in 1788, but never completed. It has remained the most widely current book in our colonial literature. *Poor Richard's Almanac*, begun in 1732 and continued for about twenty-five years, had an annual circulation of ten thousand copies. It was filled with proverbial sayings in prose and verse, inculcating the virtues of industry, honesty, and frugality.* Some of these were original with Franklin, others were selected from the proverbial wisdom of the ages, but a new force was given

* *The Way to Wealth, Plan for Saving One Hundred Thousand Pounds, Rules of Health, Advice to a Young Tradesman, The Way to Make Money Plenty in Every Man's Pocket, etc.*

them by pungent turns of expression. Poor Richard's saws were such as these: "Little strokes fell great oaks;" "Three removes are as bad as a fire;" "Early to bed and early to rise makes a man healthy, wealthy, and wise;" "Never leave that till to-morrow which you can do to-day;" "What maintains one vice would bring up two children;" "It is hard for an empty bag to stand upright."

Now and then there are truths of a higher kind than these in Franklin, and Sainte Beuve, the great French critic, quotes, as an example of his occasional finer moods, the saying, "Truth and sincerity have a certain distinguishing native luster about them which cannot be counterfeited; they are like fire and flame that cannot be painted." But the sage who invented the Franklin stove had no disdain of small utilities; and in general the last word of his philosophy is well expressed in a passage of his *Autobiography:* "Human felicity is produced not so much by great pieces of good fortune, that seldom happen, as by little advantages that occur every day; thus, if you teach a poor young man to shave himself and keep his razor in order, you may contribute more to the happiness of his life than in giving him a thousand guineas."

1. Captain John Smith. A True Relation of Virginia. Deane's edition. Boston: 1866.
2. Cotton Mather. Magnalia Christi Americana. Hartford: 1820.

3. Samuel Sewall. Diary. Massachusett's Historical Collections. Fifth Series. Vols. v, vi, and vii. Boston: 1878,

4. Jonathan Edwards. Eight Sermons on Various Occasions. Vol. vii. of Edwards's Words. Edited by Sereno Dwight. New York: 1829.

5. Benjamin Franklin. Autobiography. Edited by John Bigelow. Philadelphia: 1869. [J. B. Lippincott & Co.]

6. Essays and Bagatelles. Vol. ii. of Franklin's Works. Edited by David Sparks. Boston: 1836.

7. Moses Coit Tyler. A History of American Literature. 1607–1765. New York: 1878. [G. P. Putnam's Sons.]

CHAPTER II.
THE REVOLUTIONARY PERIOD.

1765-1815.

IT will be convenient to treat the fifty years which elapsed between the meeting at New York, in 1765, of a Congress of delegates from nine colonies, to protest against the Stamp Act, and the close of the second war with England, in 1815, as, for literary purposes, a single period. This half century was the formative era of the American nation. Historically it is divisible into the years of revolution and the years of construction. But the men who led the movement for independence were also, in great part, the same who guided in shaping the Constitution of the new republic, and the intellectual impress of the whole period is one and the same. The character of the age was as distinctly political as that of the colonial era—in New England at least—was theological; and literature must still continue to borrow its interest from history. Pure literature, or what, for want of a better term we call *belles lettres*, was not born in America until the nineteenth century was well under way. It is true that the Revolution had its humor, its poetry, and even its fiction; but these were strictly for the home market. They hardly penetrated the consciousness of Europe at all, and are not to be compared with the contemporary work of English authors like Cowper and Sheridan and Burke. Their importance for us to-day is rather antiquarian than literary, though the most noteworthy of them will be mentioned in due course in the present chapter. . It is also true that one or two of Irving's early books fall within the last years of the period now under consideration. But literary epochs overlap one another at the edges, and these writings may best be postponed to a subsequent chapter.

Among the most characteristic products of the intellectual stir that preceded and accompanied the revolutionary movement, were the speeches of political orators like Samuel Adams, James Otis, and Josiah Quincy in Massachusetts, and Patrick Henry in Virginia. Oratory is the art of a free people, and as in the forensic assemblies of Greece and Rome, and in the Parliament of Great Britain, so in the conventions and congresses of revolutionary America it sprang up and flourished naturally. The age, moreover, was an eloquent, not to say a rhetorical age; and the influence of Johnson's orotund prose, of the declamatory *Letters of Junius*, and of the speeches of Burke, Fox, Sheridan, and the elder Pitt is perceptible in the debates of our early congresses. The fame of a great orator, like that of a great actor, is largely traditionary. The spoken word transferred to the printed page loses

The Revolutionary Period. 53

the glow which resided in the man and the moment. A speech is good if it attains its aim, if it moves the hearers to the end which is sought. But the fact that this end is often temporary and occasional, rather than universal and permanent, explains why so few speeches are really literature. If this is true, even where the words of an orator are preserved exactly as they were spoken, it is doubly true when we have only the testimony of contemporaries as to the effect which the oration produced. The fiery utterances of Adams, Otis, and Quincy were either not reported at all or very imperfectly reported, so that posterity can judge of them only at second hand. Patrick Henry has fared better, many of his orations being preserved in substance, if not in the letter, in Wirt's biography. Of these the most famous was the defiant speech in the Convention of Delegates, March 28, 1775, throwing down the gauge of battle to the British ministry. The ringing sentences of this challenge are still declaimed by school boys, and many of them remain as familiar as household words. "I have but one lamp by which my feet are guided, and that is the lamp of experience. I know of no way of judging of the future but by the past. . . . Gentlemen may cry peace, peace, but there is no peace. . . . Is life so dear, or peace so sweet, as to be purchased at the price of chains and slavery! Forbid it, Almighty God! I know not what course others may take, but as for me, give me liberty, or give me death!" The eloquence of Patrick Henry was fervid rather than weighty or rich. But if such specimens of the oratory of the American patriots as have come down to us fail to account for the wonderful impression that their words are said to have produced upon their fellow-countrymen, we should remember that they are at a disadvantage when read instead of heard. The imagination should supply all those accessories which gave them vitality when first pronounced: the living presence and voice of the speaker; the listening Senate; the grave excitement of the hour and of the impending conflict. The wordiness and exaggeration; the highly latinized diction; the rhapsodies about freedom which hundreds of Fourth-of-July addresses have since turned into platitudes—all these coming hot from the lips of men whose actions in the field confirmed the earnestness of their speech —were effective enough in the crisis and for the purpose to which they were addressed.

The press was an agent in the cause of liberty no less potent than the platform, and patriots such as Adams, Otis, Quincy, Warren, and Hancock wrote constantly for the newspapers essays and letters on the public questions of the time signed "Vindex," "Hyperion," "Independent," "Brutus," "Cassius," and the like, and couched in language which to the taste of to-day seems rather over rhetorical. Among the most important of these political essays were the *Circular Letter to each Colonial Legislature*, published by Adams and Otis in 1768; Quincy's *Observations on the Boston Port Bill*, 1774, and Otis's *Rights of the British Colonies*, a pamphlet of one hundred and twenty pages, printed in 1764. No collection of Otis's writings has ever been made. The life of Quincy, published by his son, preserves for posterity his journals and correspondence, his newspaper essays, and his speeches at the bar, taken from the Massachusetts law reports.

Among the political literature which is of perennial interest to the American people are such State documents as the Declaration of Independence, the Constitution of the United States, and the messages, inaugural addresses, and other writings of our early presidents. Thomas Jefferson, the third president of the United States, and the father of the Democratic party, was the author of the Declaration of Independence, whose opening sentences have become commonplaces in the memory of all readers. One sentence in particular has been as a shibboleth, or war-cry, or declaration of faith among Democrats of all shades of opinion: "We hold these truths to be self-evident: that all men are created equal; that they are endowed by their Creator with certain unalienable rights; that among these are life, liberty, and the pursuit of happiness." Not so familiar to modern readers is the following, which an English historian of our literature calls "the most eloquent clause of that great document," and "the most interesting suppressed passage in American literature." Jefferson was a southerner, but even at that early day the South had grown sensitive on the subject of slavery, and Jefferson's arraignment of King George for promoting the "peculiar institution" was left out from the final draft of the Declaration in deference to southern members.

"He has waged cruel war against human nature itself, violating its most sacred rights of life and liberty, in the persons of a distant people who never offended him, captivating and carrying them into slavery in another hemisphere, or to incur miserable death in their transportation thither. This piratical warfare, the opprobrium of infidel powers, is the warfare of the Christian king of Great Britain. Determined to keep open a market where men should be bought and sold, he has prostituted his negative by suppressing every legislative attempt to restrain this execrable commerce. And, that this assemblage of horrors might want no fact of distinguished dye, he is now exciting those very people to rise in arms against us, and purchase that liberty of which he deprived them by murdering the people upon whom he obtruded them, and thus paying off former crimes committed against the liberties of one people by crimes which he urges them to commit against the lives of another."

The tone of apology or defense which Calhoun and other southern statesmen afterward adopted on the subject of slavery was not taken by the men of Jefferson's generation. Another famous

Virginian, John Randolph of Roanoke, himself a slaveholder, in his speech on the militia bill in the House of Representatives, December 10, 1811, said : "I speak from facts when I say that the night-bell never tolls for fire in Richmond that the mother does not hug her infant more closely to her bosom." This was said *apropos* of the danger of a servile insurrection in the event of a war with England—a war which actually broke out in the year following, but was not attended with the slave rising which Randolph predicted. Randolph was a thorough-going "States rights" man, and though opposed to slavery on principle, he cried hands off to any interference by the General Government with the domestic institutions of the States. His speeches *read* better than most of his contemporaries'. They are interesting in their exhibit of a bitter and eccentric individuality, witty, incisive, and expressed in a pungent and familiar style which contrasts refreshingly with the diplomatic language and glittering generalities of most congressional oratory, whose verbiage seems to keep its subject always at arm's length.

Another noteworthy writing of Jefferson's was his Inaugural Address of March 4, 1801, with its programme of "equal and exact justice to all men, of whatever state or persuasion, religious or political; peace, commerce, and honest friendship with all nations, entangling alliances with none; the support of the State governments in all their rights; . . . absolute acquiescence in the decisions of the majority; . . . the supremacy of the civil over the military authority; economy in the public expense; freedom of religion, freedom of the press, and freedom of person under the protection of the *habeas corpus*, and trial by juries impartially selected."

During his six years' residence in France, as American Minister, Jefferson had become indoctrinated with the principles of French democracy. His main service and that of his party—the Democratic or, as it was then called, the Republican party—to the young republic was in its insistence upon toleration of all beliefs and upon the freedom of the individual from all forms of governmental restraint. Jefferson has some claims to rank as an author in general literature. Educated at William and Mary College in the old Virginia capital, Williamsburg, he became the founder of the University of Virginia, in which he made special provision for the study of Anglo-Saxon, and in which the liberal scheme of instruction and discipline was conformed, in theory at least, to the "university idea." His *Notes on Virginia* are not without literary quaility, and one description, in particular, has been often quoted—the passage of the Potomac through the Blue Ridge—in which is this poetically imaginative touch : " The mountain being cloven asunder, she presents to your eye, through the cleft, a small catch of smooth blue horizon, at an infinite distance in the plain country, inviting you, as it were, from the riot and

THE REVOLUTIONARY PERIOD.   59

tumult roaring around, to pass through the breach and participate of the calm below."

After the conclusion of peace with England, in 1783, political discussion centered about the Constitution, which in 1788 took the place of the looser Articles of Confederation adopted in 1778. The Constitution as finally ratified was a compromise between two parties—the Federalists, who wanted a strong central government, and the Anti-Federals (afterward called Republicans, or Democrats), who wished to preserve State sovereignty. The debates on the adoption of the Constitution, both in the General Convention of the States, which met at Philadelphia in 1787, and in the separate State Conventions called to ratify its action, form a valuable body of comment and illustration upon the instrument itself. One of the most notable of the speeches in opposition was Patrick Henry's address before the Virginia Convention. "That this is a consolidated government," he said, " is demonstrably clear; and the danger of such a government is, to my mind, very striking." The leader of the Federal party was Alexander Hamilton, the ablest constructive intellect among the statesmen of our revolutionary era, of whom Talleyrand said that he "had never known his equal;" whom Guizot classed with "the men who have best known the vital principles and fundamental conditions of a government worthy of its name and mission." Hamilton's speech *On the Expediency of Adopting the Federal Constitution*, delivered in the Convention of New York, June 24, 1788, was a masterly statement of the necessity and advantages of the Union. But the most complete exposition of the constitutional philosophy of the Federal party was the series of eighty-five papers entitled the *Federalist*, printed during the years 1787–88, and mostly in the *Independent Journal* of New York, over the signature "*Publius.*" These were the work of Hamilton, of John Jay, afterward Chief Justice, and of James Madison, afterward President of the United States. The *Federalist* papers, though written in a somewhat ponderous diction, are among the great landmarks of American history, and were in themselves a political education to the generation that read them. Hamilton was a brilliant and versatile figure, a persuasive orator, a forcible writer, and as Secretary of the Treasury under Washington the foremost of American financiers. He was killed, in a duel, by Aaron Burr, at Hoboken, in 1804.

The Federalists were victorious, and under the provisions of the new Constitution George Washington was inaugurated first President of the United States, on March 4, 1789. Washington's writings have been collected by Jared Sparks. They consist of journals, letters, messages, addresses, and public documents, for the most part plain and business-like in manner, and without any literary pretensions. The most elaborate and the best known of them is his *Farewell Address*, issued on his retirement from the presidency in 1796. In the composition of this he was assisted by Madison, Hamilton, and Jay. It is wise in substance and dignified, though somewhat stilted in expression. The correspondence of John Adams, second President of the United States, and his diary, kept from 1755–85, should also be mentioned as important sources for a full knowledge of this period.

In the long life-and-death struggle of Great Britain against the French Republic and its successor, Napoleon Bonaparte, the Federalist party in this country naturally sympathized with England, and the Jeffersonian Democracy with France. The Federalists, who distrusted the sweeping abstractions of the French Revolution, and clung to the conservative notions of a checked and balanced freedom, inherited from English precedent, were accused of monarchical and aristocratic leanings. On their side they were not slow to accuse their adversaries of French atheism and French Jacobinism. By a singular reversal of the natural order of things the strength of the Federalist party was in New England, which was socially democratic, while the strength of the Jeffersonians was in the South, whose social structure — owing to the system of slavery — was intensely aristocratic. The war of 1812 with England was so unpopular in New England, by reason of the injury which it threatened to inflict on its commerce, that the Hartford Convention of 1814 was more than suspected of a design to bring about the secession of New England from the Union. A good deal of oratory was called out by the debates on the commercial treaty with Great Britain, negotiated by Jay in 1795, by the Alien and Sedition Law of 1798, and by other pieces of Federalist legislation, previous to the downfall of that party and the election of Jefferson to the presidency in 1800. The best of the Federalist orators during those years was Fisher Ames, of Massachusetts, and the best of his orations was, perhaps, his speech on the British treaty in the House of Representatives, April 18, 1796. The speech was, in great measure, a protest against American chauvinism and the violation of international obligations. "It has been said the world ought to rejoice if Britain was sunk in the sea; if where there are now men and wealth and laws and liberty, there was no more than a sand bank for sea-monsters to fatten on; space for the storms of the ocean to mingle in conflict. . . . What is patriotism? Is it a narrow affection for the spot where a man was born? Are the very clods where we tread entitled to this ardent preference because they are greener? . . . I see no exception to the respect that is paid among nations to the law of good faith. . . . It is observed by barbarians—a whiff of tobacco smoke or a string of beads gives not merely binding force but sanctity to treaties. Even in Algiers a truce may be bought for money, but, when ratified, even Algiers is too wise or too just to disown and annul its obligation." Ames was a scholar, and his speeches are more finished and thoughtful, more *literary*, in a way, than those of his contemporaries. His eulogiums on Washington and Hamilton are elaborate tributes, rather excessive, perhaps, in laudation and in classical allusions. In all the oratory of the revolutionary period there is nothing equal in deep and condensed energy of feeling to the single clause in Lincoln's Gettysburg Address, "that we here highly resolve that these dead shall not have died in vain."

A prominent figure during and after the War of the Revolution was Thomas Paine, or, as he was somewhat disrespectfully called, "Tom Paine." He was a dissenting minister who, conceiving himself ill treated by the British Government, came to Philadelphia in 1774 and threw himself heart and soul into the colonial cause. His pamphlet, *Common Sense*, issued in 1776, began with the famous words: "These are the times that try men's souls." This was followed by the *Crisis*, a series of political essays advocating independence and the establishment of a republic, published in periodical form, though at irregular intervals. Paine's rough and vigorous advocacy was of great service to the American patriots. His writings were popular and his arguments were of a kind easily understood by plain people, addressing themselves to the common sense, the prejudices and passions of unlettered readers. He afterward went to France and took an active part in the popular movement there, crossing swords with Burke in his *Rights of Man*, 1791-92, written in defense of the French Revolution. He was one of the two foreigners who sat in the Convention; but falling under suspicion during the days of the terror, he was committed to the prison of the Luxembourg and only released upon the fall of Robespierre July 27, 1794. While in prison he wrote a portion of his best known work, the *Age of Reason*. This appeared in two parts in 1794 and 1795, the manuscript of the first part having been intrusted to Joel Barlow, the American poet, who happened to be in Paris when Paine was sent to prison.

The *Age of Reason* damaged Paine's reputation in America, where the name of "Tom Paine" became a stench in the nostrils of the godly and a synonym for atheism and blasphemy. His book was denounced from a hundred pulpits, and copies of it were carefully locked away from the sight of "the young," whose religious beliefs it might undermine. It was, in effect, a crude and popular statement of the Deistic argument against Christianity. What the cutting logic and persiflage—the *sourire hideux*—of Voltaire had done in France, Paine, with coarser materials, essayed to do for the English-speaking populations. Deism was in the air of the time; Franklin, Jefferson, Ethan Allen, Joel Barlow, and other prominent Americans were openly or unavowedly deistic. Free thought, somehow, went along with democratic opinions, and was a part of the liberal movement of the age. Paine was a man without reverence, imagination, or religious feeling. He was no scholar, and he was not troubled by any perception of the deeper and subtler aspects of the questions which he touched. In his examination of the Old and New Testaments, he insisted that the Bible was an imposition and a forgery, full of lies, absurdities, and obscenities. Supernatural Christianity, with all its mysteries and miracles, was a fraud practiced by priests upon the people, and churches were instruments of oppression in the hands of tyrants. This way of accounting for Christianity would not now be accepted by even the most "advanced" thinkers. The contest between skepticism and revelation has long since shifted to other grounds. Both the philosophy and the temper of the *Age of Reason* belong to the eighteenth century. But Paine's downright pugnacious method of attack was effective with shrewd, half-educated doubters, and in America well-thumbed copies of his book passed from hand to hand in many a rural tavern or store, where the village atheist wrestled in debate with the deacon or the school-master. "When one part of God," exclaims Paine—to give an instance of the method and spirit of his book— "is represented as a dying man, and another part called the Holy Ghost, by a flying pigeon, it is impossible that belief can attach itself to such wild conceits. The book called the Book of Matthew says that *the Holy Ghost descended in the shape of a dove.* It might as well have said a goose; the creatures are equally harmless, and the one is as much a nonsensical lie as the other."

And again: "What is it the Testament teaches us?—to believe that the Almighty committed debauchery with a woman engaged to be married! And the belief of this debauchery is called faith."

When we turn from the political and controversial writings of the Revolution to such lighter literature as existed, we find little that would deserve mention in a more crowded period. The few things in this kind that have kept afloat on the current of time—*rari nantes in gurgite vasto*—attract attention rather by reason of their fewness than of any special excellence that they have. During the eighteenth century American literature continued to accommodate itself to changes of taste in the old country. The so-called classical or Augustan writers of the reign of Queen Anne replaced other models of style: the *Spectator* set the fashion of almost all of our lighter prose, from Franklin's *Busybody* down to the time of Irving, who perpetuated the Addisonian tradition later than any English writer. The influence of Locke, of Dr. Johnson, and of the Parliamentary orators has already been mentioned. In poetry the example of Pope was dominant, so that we find, for example, William Livingston, who became governor of New Jersey and a member of the Continental Congress, writing in 1747 a poem on *Philosophic Solitude* which reproduces the trick of Pope's antitheses and climaxes with the imagery of the *Rape of the Lock*, and the didactic morality of the *Imitations from Horace* and the *Moral Essays*:

"Let ardent heroes seek renown in arms,
Pant after fame and rush to war's alarms;
To shining palaces let fools resort
And dunces cringe to be esteemed at court.
Mine be the pleasure of a rural life,
From noise remote and ignorant of strife,
Far from the painted belle and white-gloved beau,
The lawless masquerade and midnight show;
From ladies, lap-dogs, courtiers, garters, stars,
Fops, fiddlers, tyrants, emperors, and czars."

The most popular poem of the Revolutionary period was John Trumbull's *McFingal*, published in part at Philadelphia in 1775, and in complete shape at Hartford in 1782. It went through more than thirty editions in America, and was several times reprinted in England. *McFingal* was a satire in four cantos, directed against the American Loyalists, and modeled quite closely upon Butler's mock heroic poem, *Hudibras*. As Butler's hero sallies forth to put down May games and bear-baitings, so the tory McFingal goes out against the liberty-poles and bon-fires of the patriots, but is tarred and feathered, and otherwise ill entreated, and finally takes refuge in the camp of General Gage at Boston. The poem is written with smartness and vivacity, attains often to drollery and sometimes to genuine humor. It remains one of the best of American political satires, and unquestionably the most successful of the many imitations of *Hudibras*, whose manner it follows so closely that some of its lines, which have passed into currency as proverbs, are generally attribued to Butler. For example:

> "No man e'er felt the halter draw
> With good opinion of the law."

Or this:

> "For any man with half an eye
> What stands before him may espy;
> But optics sharp it needs, I ween,
> To see what is not to be seen."

Trumbull's wit did not spare the vulnerable points of his own countrymen, as in his sharp skit at slavery in the couplet about the newly adopted flag of the Confederation:

> "Inscribed with inconsistent types
> Of Liberty and thirteen stripes."

Trumbull was one of a group of Connecticut literati, who made much noise in their time as the "Hartford Wits." The other members of the group were Lemuel Hopkins, David Humphreys, Joel Barlow, Elihu Smith, Theodore Dwight, and Richard Alsop. Trumbull, Humphreys, and Barlow had formed a friendship and a kind of literary partnership at Yale, where they were contemporaries of each other and of Timothy Dwight. During the war they served in the army in various capacities, and at its close they found themselves again together for a few years at Hartford, where they formed a club that met weekly for social and literary purposes. Their presence lent a sort of *éclat* to the little provincial capital, and their writings made it for a time an intellectual center quite as important as Boston or Philadelphia or New York. The Hartford Wits were staunch Federalists, and used their pens freely in support of the administrations of Washington and Adams, and in ridicule of Jefferson and the Democrats. In 1786-87 Trumbull, Hopkins, Barlow, and Humphreys published in the *New Haven Gazette* a series of satirical papers entitled the *Anarchiad*, suggested by the English *Rolliad*, and purporting to be extracts from an ancient epic on "the Restoration of Chaos and Substantial Night." These papers were an effort to correct, by ridicule, the anarchic condition of things which preceded the adoption of the Federal Constitution in 1789. It was a time of great confusion and discontent, when, in parts of the country, Democratic mobs were protesting against the vote of five years' pay by the Continental Congress to the officers of the American army. The *Anarchiad* was followed by the *Echo* and the *Political Green House*, written mostly by Alsop and Theodore Dwight, and similar in character and tendency to the earlier series. Time has greatly blunted the edge of these satires, but they were influential in their day, and are an important part of the literature of the old Federalist party.

Humphreys became afterward distinguished in the diplomatic service, and was, successively, embassador to Portugal and to Spain, whence he introduced into America the breed of merino sheep. He had been on Washington's staff during the war, and was several times an inmate of his house at Mount Vernon, where he produced, in 1785, the best known of his writings, *Mount Vernon*, an ode of a rather mild description, which once had admirers. Joel Barlow cuts a larger figure in contemporary letters. After leaving Hartford, in 1788, he went to France, where he resided for seventeen years, made a fortune in speculations, and became imbued with French principles, writing a song in praise of the Guillotine, which gave great scandal to his old friends at home. In 1805 he returned to America, and built a fine residence near Washington, which he called Kalorama. Barlow's literary fame, in his own generation, rested upon his prodigious epic, the *Columbiad*. The first form of this was the *Vision of Columbus*, published at Hartford in 1787. This he afterward recast and enlarged into the *Columbiad*, issued in Philadelphia in 1807, and dedicated to Robert Fulton, the inventor of the steamboat. This was by far the most sumptuous piece of book-making that had then been published in America, and was embellished with plates executed by the best London engravers.

The *Columbiad* was a grandiose performance, and has been the theme of much ridicule by later writers. Hawthorne suggested its being dramatized, and put on to the accompaniment of artillery and thunder and lightning; and E. P. Whipple declared that "no critic in the last fifty years had read more than a hundred lines of it." In its ambitiousness and its length it was symptomatic of the spirit of the age which was patriotically determined to create, by *tour de force*, a national literature of a size commensurate with the scale of American nature and the destinies of the republic. As America was bigger than Argos and Troy, we ought to have a bigger epic than the *Iliad*. Accordingly, Barlow makes Hesper fetch Columbus from his prison to a "hill of vision," where he unrolls before his eye a panorama of the history of America, or, as our bards then preferred to call it, Columbia. He shows him the conquest of Mexico by Cortez; the rise and fall of the kingdom of the Incas in Peru; the settlements of the English Colonies in North America; the old French and Indian Wars; the Revolution, ending with a prophecy of the future greatness of the new-born nation. The machinery of the *Vision* was borrowed from the 11th and 12th books of *Paradise Lost*. Barlow's verse was the ten-syllabled rhyming couplet of Pope, and his poetic style was distinguished by the vague, glittering imagery and the false sublimity which marked the epic attempts of the Queen Anne poets. Though Barlow was but a masquerader in true heroic, he showed himself a true poet in mock heroic. His *Hasty Pudding*, written in Savoy in 1793, and dedicated to Mrs. Washington, was thoroughly American. in subject at least, and its humor, though over-elaborate, is good. One couplet in particular has prevailed against oblivion :

> " E'en in thy native regions how I blush
> To hear the Pennsylvanians call thee *Mush!*"

Another Connecticut poet—one of the seven who were fondly named "The Pleiads of Connecticut" – was Timothy Dwight, whose *Conquest of Canaan*, written shortly after his graduation from college, but not published till 1785, was, like the *Columbiad*, an experiment toward the domestication of the epic muse in America. It was written like Barlow's poem, in rhymed couplets, and the patriotic impulse of the time shows oddly in the introduction of our Revolutionary War, by way of episode, among the wars of Israel. *Greenfield Hill*, 1794, was an idyllic and moralizing poem, descriptive of a rural parish in Connecticut of which the author was for a time the pastor. It is not quite without merit; shows plainly the influence of Goldsmith, Thomson, and Beattie, but as a whole is tedious and tame. Byron was amused that there should have been an American poet christened Timothy, and it is to be feared that amusement would have been the chief emotion kindled in the breast of the wicked Voltaire had he ever chanced to see the stern dedication to himself of the same poet's *Triumph of Infidelity*, 1788. Much more important than Dwight's poetry was his able *Theology Explained and Defended*, 1794, a restatement, with modifications, of the Calvinism of Jonathan Edwards, which was accepted by the Congregational churches of New England as an authoritative exponent of the orthodoxy of the time. His *Travels in New England and New York*, including descriptions of Niagara, the White Mountains, Lake George, the Catskills, and other passages of natural scenery, not so familiar then as now, was published posthumously in 1821, was praised by Southey, and is still readable. As President of Yale College from 1795 to 1817, Dwight, by his learning and ability, his sympathy with young men, and the force and dignity of his character, exerted a great influence in the community.

The strong political bias of the time drew into its vortex most of the miscellaneous literature that was produced. A number of ballads, serious and comic, Whig and Tory, dealing with the battles and other incidents of the long war, enjoyed a wide circulation in the newspapers, or were hawked about in printed broadsides. Most of these have no literary merit, and are now mere antiquarian curiosities. A favorite piece on the Tory side was the *Cow Chase*, a cleverish parody on *Chevy Chase*, written by the gallant and unfortunate Major Andre, at the expense of "Mad" Anthony Wayne. The national song *Yankee Doodle* was evolved during the Revolution, and, as is the case with *John Brown's Body* and many other popular melodies, some obscurity hangs about its origin. The air was an old one, and the words of the chorus seem to have been adapted or corrupted from a Dutch song, and applied in derision to the Provincials by the soldiers of the British army as early as 1755. Like many another nickname, the term Yankee Doodle was taken up by the nicknamed and proudly made their own. The stanza,

"Yankee Doodle came to town," etc.,

antedates the war; but the first complete set of words to the tune was the *Yankee's Return from Camp*, which is apparently of the year 1775. The most popular humorous ballad on the Whig side was the *Battle of the Kegs*, founded on a laughable incident of the campaign at Philadelphia. This was written by Francis Hopkinson, a Philadelphian, and one of the signers of the Declaration of Independence. Hopkinson has some title to rank as one of the earliest American humorists. Without the keen wit of *McFingal* some of his *Miscellaneous Essays and Occasional Writings*, published in 1792, have more geniality and heartiness than Trumbull's satire. His *Letter on Whitewashing* is a bit of domestic humor that foretokens the *Danbury News* man, and his *Modern Learning*, 1784, a burlesque on college examinations, in which a salt-box is described from the point of view of metaphysics, logic, natural philosophy, mathematics, anatomy, surgery and chemistry, long kept its place in school-readers and other collections. His son, Joseph Hopkinson, wrote the song of *Hail Columbia*, which is saved from insignificance only by the music to which it was married,

the then popular air of "The President's March."
The words were written in 1798, on the eve of a
threatened war with France, and at a time when
party spirit ran high. It was sung nightly by
crowds in the streets, and for a whole season by a
favorite singer at the theater; for by this time
there were theaters in Philadelphia, in New York,
and even in Puritanic Boston. Much better than
Hail Columbia was the *Star Spangled Banner*, the
words of which were composed by Francis Scott
Key, a Marylander, during the bombardment by
the British of Fort McHenry, near Baltimore, in
1812. More pretentious than these was the once
celebrated ode of Robert Treat Paine, Jr., *Adams
and Liberty*, recited at an anniversary of the Massachusetts Charitable Fire Society. The sale of
this is said to have netted its author over $750, but
it is, notwithstanding, a very wooden performance.
Paine was a young Harvard graduate, who had
married an actress playing at the old Federal
Street Theater, the first play-house opened in
Boston, in 1794. His name was originally Thomas,
but this was changed for him by the Massachusetts Legislature, because he did not wish to be
confounded with the author of the *Age of Reason*.
"Dim are those names erstwhile in battle loud,"
and many an old Revolutionary worthy who fought
for liberty with sword and pen is now utterly forgotten, or consigned to the limbo of Duyckinck's
Cyclopedia and Griswold's *Poets of America*. Here
and there a line has, by accident, survived to do

duty as a motto or inscription, while all its context is buried in oblivion. Few have read any thing more of Jonathan M. Sewall's, for example, than the couplet,

> "No pent-up Utica contracts your powers,
> But the whole boundless continent is yours,"

taken from his *Epilogue to Cato*, written in 1778.

Another Revolutionary poet was Philip Freneau; "that rascal Freneau," as Washington called him, when annoyed by the attacks upon his administration in Freneau's *National Gazette*. He was of Huguenot descent, was a classmate of Madison at Princeton College, was taken prisoner by the British during the war, and when the war was over, engaged in journalism, as an ardent supporter of Jefferson and the Democrats. Freneau's patriotic verses and political lampoons are now unreadable; but he deserves to rank as the first real American poet, by virtue of his *Wild Honeysuckle*, *Indian Burying Ground*, *Indian Student*, and a few other little pieces, which exhibit a grace and delicacy inherited, perhaps, with his French blood.

Indeed, to speak strictly, all of the "poets" hitherto mentioned were nothing but rhymers; but in Freneau we meet with something of beauty and artistic feeling; something which still keeps his verses fresh. In his treatment of Indian themes, in particular, appear for the first time a sense of the picturesque and poetic elements in the character and wild life of the red man, and that pensive sentiment which the fading away of the tribes toward the sunset has left in the wake of their retreating footsteps. In this Freneau anticipates Cooper and Longfellow, though his work is slight compared with the *Leatherstocking Tales* or *Hiawatha*. At the time when the Revolutionary War broke out the population of the colonies was over three millions; Philadelphia had thirty thousand inhabitants, and the frontier had retired to a comfortable distance from the sea-board. The Indian had already grown legendary to town dwellers, and Freneau fetches his *Indian Student* not from the outskirts of the settlement, but from the remote backwoods of the State:

> "From Susquehanna's farthest springs,
>   Where savage tribes pursue their game
> (His blanket tied with yellow strings),
>   A shepherd of the forest came."

Campbell " lifted "—in his poem *O'Conor's Child* —the last line of the following stanza from Freneau's *Indian Burying Ground*:

> "By midnight moons, o'er moistening dews,
>   In vestments for the chase arrayed,
> The hunter still the deer pursues—
>   The hunter and the deer a shade."

And Walter Scott did Freneau the honor to borrow, in *Marmion*, the final line of one of the stanzas of his poem on the battle of Eutaw Springs:

> "They saw their injured country's woe,
> The flaming town, the wasted field;
> Then rushed to meet the insulting foe;
> They took the spear, but left the shield."

Scott inquired of an American gentleman who visited him the authorship of this poem, which he had by heart, and pronouced it as fine a thing of the kind as there was in the language.

The American drama and American prose fiction had their beginnings during the period now under review. A company of English players came to this country in 1752 and made the tour of many of the principal towns. The first play acted here by professionals on a public stage was the *Merchant of Venice*, which was given by the English company at Williamsburg, Va., in 1752. The first regular theater building was at Annapolis, Md., where in the same year this troupe performed, among other pieces, Farquhar's *Beaux' Stratagem*. In 1753 a theater was built in New York, and one in 1759 in Philadelphia. The Quakers of Philadelphia and the Puritans of Boston were strenuously opposed to the acting of plays, and in the latter city the players were several times arrested during the performances, under a Massachusetts law forbidding dramatic performances. At Newport, R. I., on the other hand, which was a health resort for planters from the Southern States and the West Indies, and the largest slave-market in the North, the actors were hospitably received. The first play known to have been written by an American was the *Prince of Parthia*, 1765, a closet drama, by Thomas Godfrey, of Philadelphia. The first play by an American writer, acted by professionals in a public theater, was Royal Tyler's *Contrast*, performed in New York in 1786. The former of these was very high tragedy, and the latter very low comedy; and neither of them is otherwise remarkable than as being the first of a long line of indifferent dramas. There is, in fact, no American dramatic literature worth speaking of; not a single American play of even the second rank, unless we except a few graceful parlor comedies, like Mr. Howell's *Elevator* and *Sleeping-Car*. Royal Tyler, the author of the *Contrast*, cut quite a figure in his day as a wit and journalist, and eventually became Chief Justice of Vermont. His comedy, the *Georgia Spec*, 1797, had a great run in Boston, and his *Algerine Captive*, published in the same year, was one of the earliest American novels. It was a rambling tale of adventure, constructed somewhat upon the plan of Smollett's novels and dealing with the piracies which led to the war between the United States and Algiers in 1815.

Charles Brockden Brown, the first American novelist of any note, was also the first professional man of letters in this country who supported himself entirely by his pen. He was born in Philadelphia in 1771, lived a part of his life in New York and part in his native city, where he started, in 1803, the *Literary Magazine and American Register*. During the years 1798-1801 he published in rapid succession six romances, *Wieland, Ormond, Arthur Mervyn, Edgar Huntley, Clara Howard*, and *Jane Talbot*. Brown was an invalid and something of a recluse, with a relish for the ghastly in incident and the morbid in character. He was in some points a prophecy of Poe and Hawthorne, though his art was greatly inferior to Poe's, and almost infinitely so to Hawthorne's. His books belong more properly to the contemporary school of fiction in England which preceded the "Waverley Novels"—to the class that includes Beckford's *Vathek*, Godwin's *Caleb Williams* and *St. Leon*, Mrs. Shelley's *Frankenstein*, and such "Gothic" romances as Lewis's *Monk*, Walpole's *Castle of Otranto*, and Mrs. Radcliffe's *Mysteries of Udolpho*. A distinguishing characteristic of this whole school is what we may call the clumsy-horrible. Brown's romances are not wanting in inventive power, in occasional situations that are intensely thrilling, and in subtle analysis of character; but they are fatally defective in art. The narrative is by turns abrupt and tiresomely prolix, proceeding not so much by dialogue as by elaborate dissection and discussion of motives and states of mind, interspersed with the author's reflections. The wild improbabilities of plot and the unnatural and even monstrous developments of character are in startling contrast with the old-fashioned preciseness of the language ; the conversations, when there are any, being conducted in that insipid dialect in which a fine woman was called an "elegant female." The following is a sample description of one of Brown's heroines, and is taken from his novel of *Ormond*, the leading character in which— a combination of unearthly intellect with fiendish wickedness—is thought to have been suggested by Aaron Burr: "Helena Cleves was endowed with every feminine and fascinating quality. Her features were modified by the most transient sentiments and were the seat of a softness at all times blushful and bewitching. All those graces of symmetry, smoothness and lustre, which assemble in the imagination of the painter when he calls from the bosom of her natal deep the Paphian divinity, blended their perfections in the shade, complexion, and hair of this lady." But, alas! "Helena's intellectual deficiencies could not be concealed. She was proficient in the elements of no science. The doctrine of lines and surfaces was as disproportionate with her intellects as with those of the mock-bird. She had not reasoned on the principles of human action, nor examined the structure of society. . . . She could not commune in their native dialect with the sages of Rome and Athens. . . . The constitution of nature, the attributes of its Author, the arrangement of the parts of the external universe, and the substance, modes of operation, and ultimate destiny of human intelligence were enigmas unsolved and insoluble by her."

Brown frequently raises a superstructure of mystery on a basis ludicrously weak. Thus the hero of his first novel, *Wieland* (whose father anticipates "Nemo," in Dickens's *Bleak House*, by dying of spontaneous combustion), is led on by what he mistakes for spiritual voices to kill his wife and children; and the voices turn out to be produced by the ventriloquism of one Carwin, the villain of the story. Similarly in *Edgar Huntley*, the plot turns upon the phenomena of sleep-walking. Brown had the good sense to place the scene of his romances in his own country, and the only passages in them which have now a living interest are his descriptions of wilderness scenery in *Edgar Huntley*, and his graphic account in *Arthur Mervyn* of the yellow-fever epidemic in Philadelphia in 1793. Shelley was an admirer of Brown, and his experiments in prose fiction, such as *Zastrozzi* and *St. Irvyne the Rosicrucian*, are of the same abnormal and speculative type.

Another book which falls within this period was the *Journal*, 1774, of John Woolman, a New Jersey Quaker, which has received the highest praise from Channing, Charles Lamb, and many others. "Get the writings of John Woolman by heart," wrote Lamb, "and love the early Quakers." The charm of this journal resides in its singular sweetness and innocence of feeling, the "deep inward stillness" peculiar to the people called Quakers

Apart from his constant use of certain phrases peculiar to the Friends, Woolman's English is also remarkably graceful and pure, the transparent medium of a soul absolutely sincere, and tender and humble in its sincerity. When not working at his trade as a tailor, Woolman spent his time in visiting and ministering to the monthly, quarterly, and yearly meetings of Friends, traveling on horseback to their scattered communities in the backwoods of Virginia and North Carolina, and northward along the coast as far as Boston and Nantucket. He was under a "concern" and a "heavy exercise" touching the keeping of slaves, and by his writing and speaking did much to influence the Quakers against slavery. His love went out, indeed, to all the wretched and oppressed; to sailors, and to the Indians in particular. One of his most perilous journeys was made to the settlements of Moravian Indians in the wilderness of Western Pennsylvania, at Bethlehem, and at Wehaloosing, on the Susquehanna. Some of the scruples which Woolman felt, and the quaint *naiveté* with which he expresses them, may make the modern reader smile—but it is a smile which is very close to a tear. Thus, when in England— where he died in 1772—he would not ride nor send a letter by mail-coach, because the poor post-boys were compelled to ride long stages in winter nights, and were sometimes frozen to death. "So great is the hurry in the spirit of this world, that in aiming to do business quickly and to gain wealth, the creation at this day doth loudly groan." Again, having reflected that war was caused by luxury in dress, etc., the use of dyed garments grew uneasy to him, and he got and wore a hat of the natural color of the fur. "In attending meetings, this singularity was a trial to me ... and some Friends, who knew not from what motives I wore it, grew shy of me. ... Those who spoke with me I generally informed, in a few words, that I believed my wearing it was not in my own will."

1. Representative American Orations. Edited by Alexander Johnston. New York: G. P. Putnam's Sons. 1884.
2. The Federalist. New York: Charles Scribner. 1863.
3. Notes on Virginia. By Thomas Jefferson. Boston. 1829.
4. Travels in New England and New York. By Timothy Dwight. New Haven. 1821.
5. McFingal: in Trumbull's Poetical Works. Hartford: 1820.
6. Joel Barlow's *Hasty Pudding*. Francis Hopkinson's *Modern Learning*. Philip Freneau's *Indian Student, Indian Burying-Ground,* and *White Honeysuckle:* in Vol. I. of Duyckinck's Cyclopedia of American Literature. New York: Charles Scribner. 1866.
7. Arthur Mervyn. By Charles Brockden Brown. Boston: S. G. Goodrich. 1827.
8. The Journal of John Woolman. With an

Introduction by John G. Whittier. Boston: James R. Osgood & Co. 1871.

9. American Literature. By Charles F. Richardson. New York: G. P. Putnam's Sons. 1887.

10. American Literature. By John Nichol. Edinburgh : Adam & Charles Black. 1882.

 AMERICAN LITERATURE.

CHAPTER III.
THE ERA OF NATIONAL EXPANSION.

1815-1837.

THE attempt to preserve a strictly chronological order must here be abandoned. About all the American literature in existence, that is of any value *as literature*, is the product of the past three quarters of a century, and the men who produced it, though older or younger, were still contemporaries. Irving's *Knickerbocker's History of New York*, 1809, was published within the recollection of some yet living, and the venerable poet, Richard H. Dana—Irving's junior by only four years—survived to 1879, when the youngest of the generation of writers that now occupy public attention had already won their spurs. Bryant, whose *Thanatopsis* was printed in 1816, lived down to 1878. He saw the beginnings of our national literature, and he saw almost as much of the latest phase of it as we see to-day in this year 1887. Still, even within the limits of a single life-time, there have been progress and change. And so, while it will happen that the consideration of writers a part of whose work falls between the dates at the head of this chapter may be postponed to subsequent chapters, we may in a general way follow the sequence of time.

The period between the close of the second war with England, in 1815, and the great financial crash of 1837, has been called, in language attributed to President Monroe, "the era of good feeling." It was a time of peace and prosperity, of rapid growth in population and rapid extension of territory. The new nation was entering upon its vast estates and beginning to realize its manifest destiny. The peace with Great Britain, by calling off the Canadian Indians and the other tribes in alliance with England, had opened up the North-west to settlement. Ohio had been admitted as a State in 1802; but at the time of President Monroe's tour, in 1817, Cincinnati had only seven thousand inhabitants, and half of the State was unsettled. The Ohio River flowed for most of its course through an unbroken wilderness. Chicago was merely a fort. Hitherto the emigration to the West had been sporadic; now it took on the dimensions of a general and almost a concerted exodus. This movement was stimulated in New England by the cold summer of 1816 and the late spring of 1817, which produced a scarcity of food that amounted in parts of the interior to a veritable famine. All through this period sounded the axe of the pioneer clearing the forest about his log cabin, and the rumble of the canvas-covered emigrant wagon over the primitive highways which crossed the Alleghanies

or followed the valley of the Mohawk. S. G. Goodrich, known in letters as "Peter Parley," in his *Recollections of a Lifetime*, 1856, describes the part of the movement which he had witnessed as a boy in Fairfield County, Conn.: " I remember very well the tide of emigration through Connecticut, on its way to the West, during the summer of 1817. Some persons went in covered wagons—frequently a family consisting of father, mother, and nine small children, with one at the breast—some on foot, and some crowded together under the cover, with kettles, gridirons, feather beds, crockery, and the family Bible, Watts's Psalms and Hymns, and Webster's Spelling-book—the lares and penates of the household. Others started in ox-carts, and trudged on at the rate of ten miles a day. . . . Many of these persons were in a state of poverty, and begged their way as they went. Some died before they reached the expected Canaan; many perished after their arrival from fatigue and privation; and others from the fever and ague, which was then certain to attack the new settlers. It was, I think, in 1818 that I published a small tract entitled '*Tother Side of Ohio*—that is, the other view, in contrast to the popular notion that it was the paradise of the world. It was written by Dr. Hand—a talented young physician of Berlin—who had made a visit to the West about these days. It consisted mainly of vivid but painful pictures of the accidents and incidents attending this wholesale migration. The roads over the Alleghanies, between Philadelphia and Pittsburg, were then rude, steep, and dangerous, and some of the more precipitous slopes were consequently strewn with the carcases of wagons, carts, horses, oxen, which had made shipwreck in their perilous descents."

But in spite of the hardships of the settler's life, the spirit of that time, as reflected in its writings, was a hopeful and a light-hearted one.

"Westward the course of empire takes its way,"

runs the famous line from Berkeley's poem on America. The New Englanders who removed to the Western Reserve went there to better themelves; and their children found themselves the owners of broad acres of virgin soil, in place of the stony-hill pastures of Berkshire and Litchfield. There was an attraction, too, about the wild, free life of the frontiersman, with all its perils and discomforts. The life of Daniel Boone, the pioneer of Kentucky—that "dark and bloody ground"—is a genuine romance. Hardly less picturesque was the old river life of the Ohio boatmen, before the coming of steam banished their queer craft from the water. Between 1810 and 1840 the center of population in the United States had moved from the Potomac to the neighborhood of Clarksburg, in West Virginia, and the population itself had increased from seven to seventeen millions. The gain was made partly in the East and South, but the general drift was westward. During the years now under review, the following new States were admitted, in the order named: Indiana, Mississippi, Illinois, Alabama, Maine, Missouri, Arkansas, Michigan. Kentucky and Tennessee had been made States in the last years of the eighteenth century, and Louisiana —acquired by purchase from France—in 1812.

The settlers, in their westward march, left large tracts of wilderness behind them. They took up first the rich bottom lands along the river courses, the Ohio and Miami and Licking, and later the valleys of the Mississippi and Missouri, and the shores of the great lakes. But there still remained back woods in New York and Pennsylvania, though the cities of New York and Philadelphia had each a population of more than one hundred thousand in 1815. When the Erie Canal was opened, in 1825, it ran through a primitive forest. N. P. Willis, who went by canal to Buffalo and Niagara in 1827, describes the houses and stores at Rochester as standing among the burnt stumps left by the first settlers. In the same year that saw the opening of this great water way, the Indian tribes, numbering now about one hundred and thirty thousand souls, were moved across the Mississippi. Their power had been broken by General Harrison's victory over Tecumseh at the battle of Tippecanoe, in 1811, and they were in fact mere remnants and fragments of the race which had hung upon the skirts of civilization, and disputed the advance of the white man for two centuries. It was not until some years later than this that railroads began

THE ERA OF NATIONAL EXPANSION. 91

to take an important share in opening up new country.

The restless energy, the love of adventure, the sanguine anticipation which characterized American thought at this time, the picturesque contrasts to be seen in each mushroom town where civilization was encroaching on the raw edge of the wilderness—all these found expression, not only in such well-known books as Cooper's *Pioneers*, 1823, and Irving's *Tour on the Prairies*, 1835, but in the minor literature which is read to-day, if at all, not for its own sake, but for the light that it throws on the history of national development: in such books as Paulding's story of *Westward Ho!* and his poem, *The Backwoodsman*, 1818; or as Timothy Flint's *Recollections*, 1826, and his *Geography and History of the Mississippi Valley*, 1827. It was not an age of great books, but it was an age of large ideas and expanding prospects. The new consciousness of empire uttered itself hastily, crudely, ran into buncombe, "spread-eagleism," and other noisy forms of patriotic exultation; but it was thoroughly democratic and American. Though literature—or at least the best literature of the time—was not yet emancipated from English models, thought and life, at any rate, were no longer in bondage—no longer provincial. And it is significant that the party in office during these years was the Democratic, the party which had broken most completely with conservative traditions. The famous "Monroe doctrine" was a pronunciamento of this aggressive democracy, and though the Federalists returned to power for a single term, under John Quincy Adams (1825–1829,) Andrew Jackson received the largest number of electoral votes, and Adams was only chosen by the House of Representatives in the absence of a majority vote for any one candidate. At the close of his term "Old Hickory," the hero of the people, the most characteristically democratic of our Presidents, and the first backwoodsman who entered the White House, was borne into office on a wave of popular enthusiasm. We have now arrived at the time when American literature, in the higher and stricter sense of the term, really began to have an existence. S. G. Goodrich, who settled at Hartford as a bookseller and publisher in 1818, says, in his *Recollections:* "About this time I began to think of trying to bring out original American works. . . . The general impression was that we had not, and could not have, a literature. It was the precise point at which Sidney Smith had uttered that bitter taunt in the *Edinburgh Review*, 'Who reads an American book?' . . . It was positively injurious to the commercial credit of a bookseller to undertake American works." Washington Irving (1783–1859) was the first American author whose books, as *books*, obtained recognition abroad; whose name was thought worthy of mention beside the names of English contemporary authors, like Byron, Scott, and Coleridge. He was also the first American writer whose writings are still read for their own sake. We read Mather's *Magnalia*, and Franklin's *Autobiography*, and Trumbull's *McFingal*—if we read them at all—as history, and to learn about the times or the men. But we read the *Sketch Book*, and *Knickerbocker's History of New York*, and the *Conquest of Granada* for themselves, and for the pleasure that they give as pieces of literary art.

We have arrived, too, at a time when we may apply a more cosmopolitan standard to the works of American writers, and may disregard many a minor author whose productions would have cut some figure had they come to light amid the poverty of our colonial age. Hundreds of these forgotten names, with specimens of their unread writings, are consigned to a limbo of immortality in the pages of Duyckinck's *Cyclopedia*, and of Griswold's *Poets of America* and *Prose Writers of America*. We may select here for special mention, and as most representative of the thought of their time, the names of Irving, Cooper, Webster, and Channing.

A generation was now coming upon the stage who could recall no other government in this country than the government of the United States, and to whom the Revolutionary War was but a tradition. Born in the very year of the peace, it was a part of Irving's mission, by the sympathetic charm of his writings and by the cordial recognition which he won in both countries, to allay the soreness which the second war, of 1812–15, had left between England and America. He was well fitted for the task of mediator. Conservative by nature, early drawn to the venerable worship of the Episcopal Church, retrospective in his tastes, with a preference for the past and its historic associations which, even in young America, led him to invest the Hudson and the region about New York with a legendary interest, he wrote of American themes in an English fashion, and interpreted to an American public the mellow attractiveness that he found in the life and scenery of Old England. He lived in both countries, and loved them both; and it is hard to say whether Irving is more of an English or of an American writer. His first visit to Europe, in 1804-6, occupied nearly two years. From 1815 to 1832 he was abroad continuously, and his "domicile," as the lawyers say, during these seventeen years was really in England, though a portion of his time was spent upon the continent, and several successive years in Spain, where he engaged upon the *Life of Columbus*, the *Conquest of Granada*, the *Companions of Columbus*, and the *Alhambra*, all published between 1828-32. From 1842 to 1846 he was again in Spain as American Minister at Madrid.

Irving was the last and greatest of the Addisonians. His boyish letters, signed "Jonathan Oldstyle," contributed in 1802 to his brother's newspaper, the *Morning Chronicle*, were, like Franklin's *Busybody*, close imitations of the *Spectator*. To the same family belonged his *Salmagundi* papers, 1807, a series of town-satires on New York society, written in conjunction with his brother William and with James K. Paulding. The little tales, essays, and sketches which compose the *Sketch Book* were written in England, and published in America, in periodical numbers, in 1819-20. In this, which is in some respects his best book, he still maintained that attitude of observation and spectatorship taught him by Addison. The volume had a motto taken from Burton, "I have no wife nor children, good or bad, to provide for—a mere spectator of other men's fortunes," etc.; and "The Author's Account of Himself" began in true Addisonian fashion: "I was always fond of visiting new scenes and observing strange characters and manners."

But though never violently "American," like some later writers who have consciously sought to throw off the trammels of English tradition, Irving was in a real way original. His most distinct addition to our national literature was in his creation of what has been called "the Knickerbocker legend." He was the first to make use, for literary purposes, of the old Dutch traditions which clustered about the romantic scenery of the Hudson. Col. T. W. Higginson, in his *History of the United States*, tells how "Mrs. Josiah Quincy, sailing up that river in 1786, when Irving was a child three years old, records that the captain of the sloop had a legend, either supernatural or traditional, for every scene, 'and not a mountain reared its head unconnected with some marvelous story.'" The material thus at hand Irving shaped into his *Knickerbocker's History of New York*, into the immortal story of *Rip Van Winkle*, and the *Legend of Sleepy Hollow* (both published in the *Sketch Book*), and in later additions to the same realm of fiction, such as *Dolph Heyliger* in *Bracebridge Hall*, the *Money Diggers*, *Wolfert Webber*, and *Kidd the Pirate*, in the *Tales of a Traveler*, and in some of the miscellanies from the *Knickerbocker Magazine*, collected into a volume, in 1855, under the title of *Wolfert's Roost*.

The book which made Irving's reputation was his *Knickerbocker's History of New York*, 1809, a burlesque chronicle, making fun of the old Dutch settlers of New Amsterdam, and attributed, by a familiar and now somewhat threadbare device,* to a little old gentleman named Diedrich Knickerbocker, whose manuscript had come into the editor's hands. The book was gravely dedicated to the New York Historical Society, and it is said to have been quoted, as authentic history, by a certain German scholar named Goeller, in a note on a passage in Thucydides. This story, though well vouched, is hard of belief: for *Knickerbocker*, though excellent fooling, has nothing of the grave irony of Swift in his *Modest Proposal* or of Defoe in his *Short Way with Dissenters*. Its mock-heroic intention is as transparent as in Fielding's parodies of Homer, which it somewhat resembles.

* Compare Carlyle's Herr Diogenes Teufelsdröckh, in *Sartor Resartus*, the author of the famous " Clothes Philosophy."

particularly in the delightfully absurd description of the mustering of the clans under Peter Stuyvesant and the attack on the Swedish Fort Christina. *Knickerbocker's History of New York* was a real addition to the comic literature of the world; a work of genuine humor, original and vital. Walter Scott said that it reminded him closely of Swift, and had touches resembling Sterne. It is not necessary to claim for Irving's little masterpiece a place beside Gulliver's Travels and Tristram Shandy. But it was, at least, the first American book in the lighter departments of literature which needed no apology and stood squarely on its own legs. It was written, too, at just the right time. Although New Amsterdam had become New York as early as 1664, the impress of its first settlers, with their quaint conservative ways, was still upon it when Irving was a boy. The descendants of the Dutch families formed a definite element not only in Manhattan, but all up along the kills of the Hudson, at Albany, at Schenectady, in Westchester County, at Hoboken, and Communipaw, localities made familiar to him in many a ramble and excursion. He lived to see the little provincial town of his birth grow into a great metropolis, in which all national characteristics were blended together, and a tide of immigration from Europe and New England flowed over the old landmarks and obliterated them utterly.

Although Irving was the first to reveal to his countrymen the literary possibilities of their early history, it must be acknowledged that with modern American life he had little sympathy. He hated politics, and in the restless democratic movement of the time, as we have described it, he found no inspiration. This moderate and placid gentleman, with his distrust of all kinds of fanaticism, had no liking for the Puritans or for their descendants, the New England Yankees, if we may judge from his sketch of Ichabod Crane, in the *Legend of Sleepy Hollow*. His genius was reminiscent, and his imagination, like Scott's, was the historic imagination. In crude America his fancy took refuge in the picturesque aspects of the past, in "survivals" like the Knickerbocker Dutch and the Acadian peasants, whose isolated communities on the lower Mississippi he visited and described. He turned naturally to the ripe civilization of the Old World. He was our first picturesque tourist, the first "American in Europe." He rediscovered England, whose ancient churches, quiet landscapes, memory-haunted cities, Christmas celebrations, and rural festivals had for him an unfailing attraction. With pictures of these, for the most part, he filled the pages of the *Sketch Book* and *Bracebridge Hall*, 1822. Delightful as are these English sketches, in which the author conducts his readers to Windsor Castle, or Stratford-on-Avon, or the Boar's Head Tavern, or sits beside him on the box of the old English stage-coach, or shares with him the Yuletide cheer at the ancient English country house, their interest has somewhat faded.

THE ERA OF NATIONAL EXPANSION. 97

The pathos of the *Broken Heart* and the *Pride of the Village*, the mild satire of the *Art of Book Making*, the rather obvious reflections in *Westminster Abbey* are not exactly to the taste of this generation. They are the literature of leisure and retrospection; and already Irving's gentle elaboration, the refined and slightly artificial beauty of his style, and his persistently genial and sympathetic attitude have begun to pall upon readers who demand a more nervous and accented kind of writing. It is felt that a little roughness, a little harshness, even, would give relief to his pictures of life. There is, for instance, something a little irritating in the old-fashioned courtliness of his manner toward women; and one reads with a certain impatience smoothly punctuated passages like the following: "As the vine, which has long twined its graceful foliage about the oak, and been lifted by it into sunshine, will, when the hardy plant is rifted by the thunderbolt, cling round it with its caressing tendrils, and bind up its shattered boughs, so is it beautifully ordered by Providence that woman, who is the mere dependent and ornament of man in his happier hours, should be his stay and solace when smitten with sudden calamity; winding herself into the rugged recesses of his nature, tenderly supporting the drooping head, and binding up the broken heart."

Irving's gifts were sentiment and humor, with an imagination sufficiently fertile, and an observation sufficiently acute to support those two main qualities, but inadequate to the service of strong passion or subtle thinking, though his pathos, indeed, sometimes reached intensity. His humor was always delicate and kindly; his sentiment never degenerated into sentimentality. His diction was graceful and elegant—too elegant, perhaps; and in his modesty he attributed the success of his books in England to the astonishment of Englishmen that an American could write good English.

In Spanish history and legend Irving found a still newer and richer field for his fancy to work upon. He had not the analytic and philosophical mind of a great historian, and the merits of his *Conquest of Granada* and *Life of Columbus* are rather *belletristisch* than scientific. But he brought to these undertakings the same eager love of the romantic past which had determined the character of his writings in America and England, and the result—whether we call it history or romance—is at all events charming as literature. His *Life of Washington*—completed in 1859—was his *magnum opus*, and is accepted as standard authority. *Mahomet and His Successors*, 1850, was comparatively a failure. But of all Irving's biographies, his *Life of Oliver Goldsmith*, 1849, was the most spontaneous and perhaps the best. He did not impose it upon himself as a task, but wrote it from a native and loving sympathy with his subject, and it is, therefore, one of the choisest literary memoirs in the language.

THE ERA OF NATIONAL EXPANSION. 101

When Irving returned to America, in 1832, he was the recipient of almost national honors. He had received the medal of the Royal Society of Literature and the degree of D.C.L. from Oxford University, and had made American literature known and respected abroad. In his modest home at Sunnyside, on the banks of the river over which he had been the first to throw the witchery of poetry and romance, he was attended to the last by the admiring affection of his countrymen. He had the love and praises of the foremost English writers of his own generation and the generation which followed—of Scott, Byron, Coleridge, Thackeray, and Dickens, some of whom had been among his personal friends. He is not the greatest of American authors, but the influence of his writings is sweet and wholesome, and it is in many ways fortunate that the first American man of letters who made himself heard in Europe should have been in all particulars a gentleman.

Connected with Irving, at least by name and locality, were a number of authors who resided in the city of New York and who are known as the Knickerbocker writers, perhaps because they were contributors to the *Knickerbocker Magazine.* One of these was James K. Paulding, a connection of Irving by marriage, and his partner in the *Salmagundi Papers.* Paulding became Secretary of the Navy under Van Buren, and lived down to the year 1860. He was a voluminous author, but his writings had no power of continuance, and are already obsolete, with the possible exception of his novel, the *Dutchman's Fireside*, 1831.

A finer spirit than Paulding was Joseph Rodman Drake, a young poet of great promise, who died in 1820, at the age of twenty-five. Drake's patriotic lyric, the *American Flag*, is certainly the most spirited thing of the kind in our poetic literature, and greatly superior to such national anthems as *Hail Columbia* and the *Star Spangled Banner*. His *Culprit Fay*, published in 1819, was the best poem that had yet appeared in America, if we except Bryant's *Thanatopsis*, which was three years the elder. The *Culprit Fay* was a fairy story, in which, following Irving's lead, Drake undertook to throw the glamour of poetry about the Highlands of the Hudson. Edgar Poe said that the poem was fanciful rather than imaginative; but it is prettily and even brilliantly fanciful, and has maintained its popularity to the present time. Such verse as the following—which seems to show that Drake had been reading Coleridge's *Christabel*, published three years before—was something new in American poetry:

> " The winds are whist and the owl is still,
>   The bat in the shelvy rock is hid,
> And naught is heard on the lonely hill,
> But the cricket's chirp and the answer shrill,
>   Of the gauze-winged katydid,
> And the plaint of the wailing whip-poor-will

> Who moans unseen, and ceaseless sings
> Ever a note of wail and woe,
> Till morning spreads her rosy wings,
> And earth and sky in her glances glow."

Here we have, at last, the whip-poor-will, an American bird, and not the conventional lark or nightingale, although the elves of the Old World seem scarcely at home on the banks of the Hudson. Drake's memory has been kept fresh not only by his own poetry, but by the beautiful elegy written by his friend Fitz-Greene Halleck, the first stanza of which is universally known:

> "Green be the turf above thee,
> Friend of my better days;
> None knew thee but to love thee,
> Nor named thee but to praise."

Halleck was born in Guilford, Connecticut, whither he retired in 1849, and resided there till his death in 1867. But his literary career is identified with New York. He was associated with Drake in writing the *Croaker Papers*, a series of humorous and satirical verses contributed in 1814 to the *Evening Post*. These were of a merely local and temporary interest; but Halleck's fine ode, *Marco Bozzaris*—though declaimed until it has become hackneyed—gives him a sure title to remembrance; and his *Alnwick Castle*, a monody, half serious and half playful on the contrasts between feudal associations and modern life, has much of that pensive lightness which characterizes Praed's best *vers de societé*.

A friend of Drake and Halleck was James Fenimore Cooper (1789–1851), the first American novelist of distinction, and, if a popularity which has endured for nearly three quarters of a century is any test, still the most successful of all American novelists. Cooper was far more intensely American than Irving, and his books reached an even wider public. " They are published as soon as he produces them," said Morse, the electrician, in 1833, "in thirty-four different places in Europe. They have been seen by American travelers in the languages of Turkey and Persia, in Constantinople, in Egypt, at Jerusalem, at Ispahan." Cooper wrote altogether too much; he published, besides his fictions, a *Naval History of the United States*, a series of naval biographies, works of travel, and a great deal of controversial matter. He wrote over thirty novels, the greater part of which are little better than trash, and tedious trash at that. This is especially true of his *tendenz* novels and his novels of society. He was a man of strongly marked individuality, fiery, pugnacious, sensitive to criticism, and abounding in prejudices. He was embittered by the scurrilous attacks made upon him by a portion of the American press, and spent a great deal of time and energy in conducting libel suits against the newspapers. In the same spirit he used fiction as a vehicle for attack upon the abuses and follies of American life. Nearly all of his novels, written with this design, are worthless. Nor was Cooper well equipped by nature and temperament for depicting character and passion in social life. Even in his best romances his heroines and his "leading juveniles "—to borrow a term from the amateur stage—are insipid and conventional. He was no satirist, and his humor was not of a high order. He was a rapid and uneven writer, and, unlike Irving, he had no style.

Where Cooper was great was in the story, in the invention of incidents and plots, in a power of narrative and description in tales of wild adventure which keeps the reader in breathless excitement to the end of the book. He originated the novel of the sea and the novel of the wilderness. He created the Indian of literature ; and in this, his peculiar field, although he has had countless imitators, he has had no equals. Cooper's experiences had prepared him well for the kingship of this new realm in the world of fiction. His childhood was passed on the borders of Otsego Lake, when central New York was still a wilderness, with boundless forests stretching westward, broken only here and there by the clearings of the pioneers. He was taken from college (Yale) when still a lad, and sent to sea in a merchant vessel, before the mast. Afterward he entered the navy and did duty on the high seas and upon Lake Ontario, then surrounded by virgin forests. He married and resigned his commission in 1811, just before the outbreak of the war with England, so that he missed the opportunity of seeing active service in any of those engagements on the ocean and our great lakes which were so glorious to American arms. But he always retained an active interest in naval affairs.

His first successful novel was *The Spy*, 1821, a tale of the Revolutionary War, the scene of which was laid in Westchester County, N. Y., where the author was then residing. The hero of this story, Harvey Birch, was one of the most skillfully drawn figures on his canvas. In 1823 he published the *Pioneers*, a work somewhat overladen with description, in which he drew for material upon his boyish recollections of frontier life at Cooperstown. This was the first of the series of five romances known as the *Leatherstocking Tales*. The others were the *Last of the Mohicans*, 1826; the *Prairie*, 1827; the *Pathfinder*, 1840; and the *Deerslayer*, 1841. The hero of this series, Natty Bumpo, or "Leatherstocking," was Cooper's one great creation in the sphere of charcter, his most original addition to the literature of the world in the way of a new human type. This backwoods philosopher—to the conception of whom the historic exploits of Daniel Boone perhaps supplied some hints; unschooled, but moved by noble impulses and a natural sense of piety and justice; passionately attached to the wilderness, and following its westering edge even unto the prairies —this man of the woods was the first real American in fiction. Hardly less individual and vital were the various types of Indian character, in Chingachgook, Uncas, Hist, and the Huron warriors. Inferior to these, but still vigorously though somewhat roughly drawn, were the waifs and strays of civilization, whom duty, or the hope of gain, or the love of adventure, or the outlawry of crime had driven to the wilderness—the solitary trapper, the reckless young frontiersman, the officers and men of out-post garrisons. Whether Cooper's Indian was the real being, or an idealized and rather melo-dramatic version of the truth, has been a subject of dispute. However this be, he has taken his place in the domain of art, and it is safe to say that his standing there is secure. No boy will ever give him up.

Equally good with the *Leatherstocking* novels, and equally national, were Cooper's tales of the sea, or at least the two best of them—the *Pilot*, 1823, founded upon the daring exploits of John Paul Jones, and the *Red Rover*, 1828. But here, though Cooper still holds the sea, he has had to admit competitors; and Britannia, who rules the waves in song, has put in some claim to a share in the domain of nautical fiction in the persons of Mr. W. Clarke Russell and others. Though Cooper's novels do not meet the deeper needs of the heart and the imagination, their appeal to the universal love of a story is perennial. We devour them when we are boys, and if we do not often return to them when we are men, that is perhaps only because we have read them before, and " know the ending." They are good yarns for the forecastle and the camp-fire; and the scholar in his study, though he may put the *Deerslayer* or the *Last of the Mohicans* away on the top-shelf, will take it down now and again, and sit up half the night over it.

Before dismissing the *belles-lettres* writings of this period, mention should be made of a few poems of the fugitive kind which seem to have taken a permanent place in popular regard. John Howard Payne, a native of Long Island, a wandering actor and playwright, who died American Consul at Tunis in 1852, wrote about 1820 for Covent Garden Theater an opera, entitled *Clari*, the libretto of which included the now famous song of *Home, Sweet Home*. Its literary pretensions were of the humblest kind, but it spoke a true word which touched the Anglo-Saxon heart in its tenderest spot, and being happily married to a plaintive air was sold by the hundred thousand, and is evidently destined to be sung forever. A like success has attended the *Old Oaken Bucket*, composed by Samuel Woodworth, a printer and journalist from Massachusetts, whose other poems, of which two collections were issued in 1818 and 1826, were soon forgotten. Richard Henry Wilde, an Irishman by birth, a gentleman of scholarly tastes and accomplishments, who wrote a great deal on Italian literature, and sat for several terms in Congress as Representative of the State of Georgia, was the author of the favorite song, *My Life is Like the Summer Rose*. Another Southerner, and a member of a distinguished Southern family, was Edward Coate Pinkney, who served nine years in the navy, and died in 1828, at the age of twenty-six, having published in 1825 a small volume of lyrical poems which had a fire and a grace uncommon at that time in American verse. One of these, *A Health*, beginning

"I fill this cup to one made up of loveliness alone,"

though perhaps somewhat overpraised by Edgar Poe, has rare beauty of thought and expression. John Quincy Adams, sixth President of the United States (1825-29), was a man of culture and of literary tastes. He published his lectures on rhetoric delivered during his tenure of the Boylston Professorship at Harvard in 1806-09; he left a voluminous diary, which has been edited since his death in 1848; and among his experiments in poetry is one of considerable merit, entitled the *Wants of Man*, an ironical sermon on Goldsmith's text:

"Man wants but little here below
Nor wants that little long."

As this poem is a curiously close anticipation of Dr. Holmes's *Contentment*, so the very popular ballad, *Old Grimes*, written about 1818, by Albert Gorton Greene, an undergraduate of Brown University in Rhode Island, is in some respects an anticipation of Holmes's quaintly pathetic *Last Leaf*.

The political literature and public oratory of

the United States during this period, although not absolutely of less importance than that which preceded and followed the Declaration of Independence and the adoption of the Constitution, demands less relative attention in a history of literature by reason of the growth of other departments of thought. The age was a political one, but no longer exclusively political. The debates of the time centered about the question of "State Rights," and the main forum of discussion was the old Senate chamber, then made illustrious by the presence of Clay, Webster, and Calhoun. The slavery question, which had threatened trouble, was put off for awhile by the Missouri Compromise of 1820, only to break out more fiercely in the debates on the Wilmot Proviso, and the Kansas and Nebraska Bill. Meanwhile the Abolition movement had been transferred to the press and the platform. Garrison started his *Liberator* in 1830, and the Antislavery Society was founded in 1833. The Whig party, which had inherited the constitutional principles of the old Federal party, advocated internal improvements at national expense and a high protective tariff. The State Rights party, which was strongest at the South, opposed these views, and in 1832 South Carolina claimed the right to "nullify" the tariff imposed by the general government. The leader of this party was John Caldwell Calhoun, a South Carolinian, who in his speech in the United States Senate, on February 13, 1832, on Nullification and the

Force Bill, set forth most authoritatively the "Carolina doctrine." Calhoun was a great debater, but hardly a great orator. His speeches are the arguments of a lawyer and a strict constitutionalist, severely logical, and with a sincere conviction in the soundness of his case. Their language is free from bad rhetoric; the reasoning is cogent, but there is an absence of emotion and imagination; they contain few quotable things, and no passages of commanding eloquence, such as strew the orations of Webster and Burke. They are not, in short, literature. Again, the speeches of Henry Clay, of Kentucky, the leader of the Whigs, whose persuasive oratory is a matter of tradition, disappoint in the reading. The fire has gone out of them.

Not so with Daniel Webster, the greatest of American forensic orators, if, indeed, he be not the greatest of all orators who have used the English tongue. Webster's speeches are of the kind that have power to move after the voice of the speaker is still. The thought and the passion in them lay hold on feelings of patriotism more lasting than the issues of the moment. It is, indeed, true of Webster's speeches, as of all speeches, that they are known to posterity more by single brilliant passages than as wholes. In oratory the occasion is of the essence of the thing, and only those parts of an address which are permanent and universal in their appeal take their place in literature. But of such detachable passages there are happily many in Webster's orations. One great thought underlay all his public life, the thought of the Union; of American nationality. What in Hamilton had been a principle of political philosophy had become in Webster a passionate conviction. The Union was his idol, and he was intolerant of any faction which threatened it from any quarter, whether the Nullifiers of South Carolina or the Abolitionists of the North. It is this thought which gives grandeur and elevation to all his utterances, and especially to the wonderful peroration of his reply to Hayne, on Mr. Foot's resolution touching the sale of the public lands, delivered in the Senate on January 26, 1830, whose closing words, "liberty and union, now and forever, one and inseparable," became the rallying cry of a great cause. Similar in sentiment was his famous speech of March 7, 1850, *On the Constitution and the Union*, which gave so much offense to the extreme Antislavery party, who held with Garrison that a Constitution which protected slavery was "a league with death and a covenant with hell." It is not claiming too much for Webster to assert that the sentences of these and other speeches, memorized and declaimed by thousands of school-boys throughout the North, did as much as any single influence to train up a generation in hatred of secession, and to send into the fields of the civil war armies of men animated with the stern resolution to fight till the last drop of blood was shed, rather than allow the Union to be dissolved.

THE ERA OF NATIONAL EXPANSION. 113

The figure of this great senator is one of the most imposing in American annals. The masculine force of his personality impressed itself upon men of a very different stamp—upon the unworldly Emerson, and upon the captious Carlyle, whose respect was not willingly accorded to any contemporary, much less to a representative of American democracy. Webster's looks and manner were characteristic. His form was massive, his skull and jaw solid, the underlip projecting, and the mouth firmly and grimly shut; his complexion was swarthy, and his black, deep set eyes, under shaggy brows, glowed with a smoldering fire. He was rather silent in society; his delivery in debate was grave and weighty, rather than fervid. His oratory was massive and sometimes even ponderous. It may be questioned whether an American orator of to-day, with intellectual abilities equal to Webster's—if such a one there were— would permit himself the use of sonorous and elaborate pictures like the famous period which follows: "On this question of principle, while actual suffering was yet afar off, they raised their flag against a power, to which, for purposes of foreign conquest and subjugation, Rome, in the height of her glory, is not to be compared; a power which has dotted over the surface of the whole globe with her possessions and military posts, whose morning drum-beat, following the sun and keeping company with the hours, circles the earth with one continuous and unbroken strain of the martial airs of England." The secret of this kind of oratory has been lost. The present generation distrusts rhetorical ornament, and likes something swifter, simpler, and more familiar in its speakers. But every thing, in declamation of this sort, depends on the way in which it is done. Webster did it supremely well; a smaller man would merely have made buncombe of it.

Among the legal orators of the time the foremost was Rufus Choate, an eloquent pleader, and, like Webster, a United States Senator from Massachusetts. Some of his speeches, though excessively rhetorical, have literary quality, and are nearly as effective in print as Webster's own. Another Massachusetts orator, Edward Everett, who in his time was successively professor in Harvard College, Unitarian minister in Boston, editor of the *North American Review*, member of both houses of Congress, Minister to England, Governor of his State, and President of Harvard, was a speaker of great finish and elegance. His addresses were mainly of the memorial and anniversary kind, and were rather lectures and Φ. B. K. prolusions than speeches. Everett was an instance of careful culture bestowed on a soil of no very great natural richness. It is doubtful whether his classical orations on Washington, the Republic, Bunker Hill Monument, and kindred themes, have enough of the breath of life in them to preserve them much longer in recollection.

New England, during these years, did not take

that leading part in the purely literary development of the country which it afterward assumed. It had no names to match against those of Irving and Cooper. Drake and Halleck—slender as was their performance in point of quantity—were better poets than the Boston bards, Charles Sprague, whose *Shakespere Ode*, delivered at the Boston theater in 1823, was locally famous; and Richard Henry Dana, whose longish narrative poem, the *Buccaneer*, 1827, once had admirers. But Boston has at no time been without a serious intellectual life of its own, nor without a circle of highly educated men of literary pursuits, even in default of great geniuses. The *North American Review*, established in 1815, though it has been wittily described as "ponderously revolving through space" for a few years after its foundation, did not exist in an absolute vacuum, but was scholarly, if somewhat heavy. Webster, to be sure, was a Massachusetts man—as were Everett and Choate—but his triumphs were won in the wider field of national politics. There was, however, a movement at this time in the intellectual life of Boston and Eastern Massachusetts, which, though not immediately contributory to the finer kinds of literature, prepared the way, by its clarifying and stimulating influences, for the eminent writers of the next generation. This was the Unitarian revolt against Puritan orthodoxy, in which William Ellery Channing was the principal leader. In a community so intensely theological as New England it was natural that any new movement in thought should find its point of departure in the churches. Accordingly, the progressive and democratic spirit of the age, which in other parts of the country took other shapes, assumed in Massachusetts the form of "liberal Christianity." Arminianism, Socinianism, and other phases of anti-Trinitarian doctrine, had been latent in some of the Congregational churches of Massachusetts for a number of years. But about 1812 the heresy broke out openly, and within a few years from that date most of the oldest and wealthiest church societies of Boston and its vicinity had gone over to Unitarianism, and Harvard College had been captured, too. In the controversy that ensued, and which was carried on in numerous books, pamphlets, sermons, and periodicals, there were eminent disputants on both sides. So far as this controversy was concerned with the theological doctrine of the Trinity, it has no place in a history of literature. But the issue went far beyond that. Channing asserted the dignity of human nature against the Calvinistic doctrine of innate depravity, and affirmed the rights of human reason and man's capacity to judge of God. "We must start in religion from our own souls," he said. And in his *Moral Argument against Calvinism*, 1820, he wrote: "Nothing is gained to piety by degrading human nature, for in the competency of this nature to know and judge of God all piety has its foundation." In opposition to Edwards's doctrine of necessity, he emphasized the freedom of the will. He maintained that the Calvinistic dogmas of original sin, foreordination, election by grace, and eternal punishment were inconsistent with the divine perfection, and made God a monster. In Channing's view the great sanction of religious truth is the moral sanction, is its agreement with the laws of conscience. He was a passionate vindicator of the liberty of the individual not only as against political oppression but against the tyranny of public opinion over thought and conscience: "We were made for free action. This alone is life, and enters into all that is good and great." This jealous love of freedom inspired all that he did and wrote. It led him to join the Antislavery party. It expressed itself in his elaborate arraignment of Napoleon in the Unitarian organ, the *Christian Examiner*, for 1827-28; in his *Remarks on Associations*, and his paper *On the Character and Writings of John Milton*, 1826. This was his most considerable contribution to literary criticism. It took for a text Milton's recently discovered *Treatise on Christian Doctrine*—the tendency of which was anti-Trinitarian—but it began with a general defense of poetry against "those who are accustomed to speak of poetry as light reading." This would now seem a somewhat superfluous introduction to an article in any American review. But it shows the nature of the *milieu* through which the liberal movement in Boston had to make its way. To assert the dignity and usefulness of the beautiful arts; to show that novels and plays and games and dances were not necessarily sinful, and might even be improving, was a part of the work of preparation done by the Unitarians in Massachusetts. People in other parts of the country had gone freely to the theater or the ball. Some people had even done so in Boston, but not with the approval of the clergy. The narrow traditions of provincial Puritanism had to be broken and a more cheerful type of religion preached before polite literature in Massachusetts could find a congenial atmosphere. In Channing's *Remarks on National Literature*, reviewing a work published in 1823, he asks the question, " Do we possess what may be called national literature?" and answers it, by implication at least, in the negative. That we do now possess a national literature, is in great part due to the influence of Channing and his associates, although his own writings, being in the main controversial and, therefore, of temporary interest, may not themselves take rank among the permanent treasures of that literature.

1. Washington Irving. Knickerbocker's History of New York. The Sketch Book. Bracebridge Hall. Tales of a Traveler. The Alhambra. Life of Oliver Goldsmith.

2. James Fenimore Cooper. The Spy. The Pilot. The Red Rover. The Leather-Stocking Tales.

3. Daniel Webster. Great Speeches and Orations. Boston : Little, Brown, & Co. 1879.

4. William Ellery Channing. The Character and Writings of John Milton. The Life and Character of Napoleon Bonaparte. Slavery. [Vols. I. and II. of the Works of William E. Channing. Boston: James Munroe & Co. 1841.]

5. Joseph Rodman Drake. The Culprit Fay. The American Flag. [Selected Poems. New York. 1835.]

6. Fitz-Greene Halleck. Marco Bozzaris. Alnwick Castle. On the Death of Drake. [Poems. New York 1827.]

CHAPTER IV.
THE CONCORD WRITERS.

1837–1861.

THERE has been but one movement in the history of the American mind which has given to literature a group of writers having coherence enough to merit the name of a school. This was the great humanitarian movement, or series of movements, in New England, which, beginning in the Unitarianism of Channing, ran through its later phase in Transcendentalism, and spent its last strength in the antislavery agitation and the enthusiasms of the Civil War. The second stage of this intellectual and social revolt was Transcendentalism, of which Emerson wrote, in 1842: "The history of genius and of religion in these times will be the history of this tendency." It culminated about 1840–41 in the establishment of the *Dial* and the Brook Farm Community, although Emerson had given the signal a few years before in his little volume entitled *Nature*, 1836, his Phi-Beta Kappa address at Harvard on the *American Scholar*, 1837, and his address in 1838 before the Divinity School at Cambridge. Ralph Waldo Emerson (1803–1882) was the prophet of the sect, and

Concord was its Mecca; but the influence of the new ideas was not confined to the little group of professed Transcendentalists; it extended to all the young writers within reach, who struck their roots deeper into the soil that it had loosened and freshened. We owe to it, in great measure, not merely Emerson, Alcott, Margaret Fuller, and Thoreau, but Hawthorne, Lowell, Whittier, and Holmes.

In its strictest sense Transcendentalism was a restatement of the idealistic philosophy, and an application of its beliefs to religion, nature, and life. But in a looser sense, and as including the more outward manifestations which drew popular attention most strongly, it was the name given to that spirit of dissent and protest, of universal inquiry and experiment, which marked the third and fourth decades of this century in America, and especially in New England. The movement was contemporary with political revolutions in Europe and with the preaching of many novel gospels in religion, in sociology, in science, education, medicine, and hygiene. New sects were formed, like the Swedenborgians, Universalists, Spiritualists, Millerites, Second Adventists, Shakers, Mormons, and Come-outers, some of whom believed in trances, miracles, and direct revelations from the divine Spirit; others in the quick coming of Christ, as deduced from the opening of the seals and the number of the beast in the Apocalypse; and still others in the reorganization of society and of the family on a different basis. New systems of education were tried, suggested by the writings of the Swiss reformer, Pestalozzi, and others. The pseudo-sciences of mesmerism and of phrenology, as taught by Gall and Spurzheim, had numerous followers. In medicine, homeopathy, hydropathy, and what Dr. Holmes calls "kindred delusions," made many disciples. Numbers of persons, influenced by the doctrines of Graham and other vegetarians, abjured the use of animal food, as injurious not only to health but to a finer spirituality. Not a few refused to vote or pay taxes. The writings of Fourier and St. Simon were translated, and societies were established where co-operation and a community of goods should take the place of selfish competition.

About the year 1840 there were some thirty of these "phalansteries" in America, many of which had their organs in the shape of weekly or monthly journals, which advocated the principle of Association. The best known of these was probably the *Harbinger*, the mouth-piece of the famous Brook Farm Community, which was founded at West Roxbury, Mass., in 1841, and lasted till 1847. The head man of Brook Farm was George Ripley, a Unitarian clergyman, who had resigned his pulpit in Boston to go into the movement, and who after its failure became and remained for many years literary editor of the *New York Tribune*. Among his associates were Charles A. Dana—now the editor of the *Sun*—Margaret Fuller, Nathaniel

Hawthorne and others not unknown to fame. The *Harbinger*, which ran from 1845 to 1849—two years after the break up of the community—had among its contributors many who were not Brook Farmers, but who sympathized more or less with the experiment. Of the number were Horace Greeley, Dr. F. H. Hedge—who did so much to introduce American readers to German literature —J. S. Dwight, the musical critic, C. P. Cranch, the poet, and younger men, like G. W. Curtis, and T. W. Higginson. A reader of to-day, looking into an odd volume of the *Harbinger*, will find in it some stimulating writing, together with a great deal of unintelligible talk about "Harmonic Unity," "Love Germination," and other matters now fallen silent. The most important literary result of this experiment at " plain living and high thinking," with its queer mixture of culture and agriculture, was Hawthorne's *Blithedale Romance*, which has for its background an idealized picture of the community life, whose heroine, Zenobia, has touches of Margaret Fuller ; and whose hero, with his hobby of prison reform, was a type of the one-idead philanthropists that abounded in such an environment. Hawthorne's attitude was always in part one of reserve and criticism, an attitude which is apparent in the reminiscences of Brook Farm in his *American Note Books*, wherein he speaks with a certain resentment of "Miss Fuller's transcendental heifer," which hooked the other cows, and was evidently to Hawthorne's mind not unsymbolic in this respect of Miss Fuller herself.

It was the day of seers and "Orphic" utterances; the air was full of the enthusiasm of humanity and thick with philanthropic projects and plans for the regeneration of the universe. The figure of the wild-eyed, long-haired reformer—the man with a panacea—the "crank" of our later terminology—became a familiar one. He abounded at non-resistance conventions and meetings of universal peace societies and of woman's rights associations. The movement had its grotesque aspects, which Lowell has described in his essay on Thoreau. "Bran had its apostles and the pre-sartorial simplicity of Adam its martyrs, tailored impromptu from the tar-pot.... Not a few impecunious zealots abjured the use of money (unless earned by other people), professing to live on the internal revenues of the spirit.... Communities were established where every thing was to be common but common sense."

This ferment has long since subsided and much of what was then seething has gone off in vapor or other volatile products. But some very solid matters also have been precipitated, some crystals of poetry translucent, symmetrical, enduring. The immediate practical outcome was disappointing, and the external history of the agitation is a record of failed experiments, spurious sciences, Utopian philosophies, and sects founded only to dwindle away or be reabsorbed into some form of orthodoxy. In the eyes of the conservative, or the worldly-minded, or of the plain people who could not understand the enigmatic utterances of the reformers, the dangerous or ludicrous sides of transcendentalism were naturally uppermost. Nevertheless the movement was but a new avatar of the old Puritan spirit; its moral earnestness, its spirituality, its tenderness for the individual conscience. Puritanism, too, in its day had run into grotesque extremes. Emerson bore about the same relation to the absurder outcroppings of transcendentalism that Milton bore to the New Lights, Ranters, Fifth Monarchy Men, etc., of his time. There is in him that mingling of idealism with an abiding sanity, and even a Yankee shrewdness, which characterizes the race. The practical, inventive, calculating, money-getting side of the Yankee has been made sufficiently obvious. But the deep heart of New England is full of dreams, mysticism, romance:

> "And in the day of sacrifice,
> When heroes piled the pyre,
> The dismal Massachusetts ice
> Burned more than others' fire."

The one element which the odd and eccentric developments of this movement shared in common with the real philosophy of transcendentalism was the rejection of authority and the appeal to the private consciousness as the sole standard of truth and right. This principle certainly lay in the ethical systems of Kant and Fichte, the great transcendentalists of Germany. It had been strongly asserted by Channing. Nay, it was the starting point of Puritanism itself, which had drawn away from the ceremonial religion of the English Church and by its Congregational system had made each church society independent in doctrine and worship. And although Puritan orthodoxy in New England had grown rigid and dogmatic, it had never used the weapons of obscurantism. By encouraging education to the utmost it had shown its willingness to submit its beliefs to the fullest discussion and had put into the hands of dissent the means with which to attack them.

In its theological aspect transcendentalism was a departure from conservative Unitarianism, as that had been from Calvinism. From Edwards to Channing, from Channing to Emerson and Theodore Parker, there was a natural and logical unfolding. Not logical in the sense that Channing accepted Edwards' premises and pushed them out to their conclusions, or that Parker accepted all of Channing's premises, but in the sense that the rigid pushing out of Edwards' premises into their conclusions by himself and his followers had brought about a moral *reductio ad absurdum* and a state of opinion against which Channing rebelled; and that Channing, as it seemed to Parker, stopped short in the carrying out of his own principles. Thus the "Channing Unitarians," while denying that Christ was God, had held that he was of divine nature, was the Son of God, and had existed before he came into the world. While rejecting the doctrine of the "Vicarious sacrifice" they maintained that Christ was a mediator and intercessor, and that his supernatural nature was testified by miracles. For Parker and Emerson it was easy to take the step to the assertion that Christ was a good and great man, divine only in the sense that God possessed him more fully than any other man known in history; that it was his preaching and example that brought salvation to men, and not any special mediation or intercession, and that his own words and acts, and not miracles, are the only and the sufficient witness to his mission. In the view of the transcendentalists Christ was as human as Buddha, Socrates or Confucius, and the Bible was but one among the "Ethnical Scriptures" or sacred writings of the peoples, passages from which were published in the transcendental organ, the *Dial*. As against these new views Channing Unitarianism occupied already a conservative position. The Unitarians as a body had never been very numerous outside of Eastern Massachusets. They had a few churches in New York and in the larger cities and towns elsewhere, but the sect, as such, was a local one. Orthodoxy made a sturdy fight against the heresy, under leaders like Leonard Woods and Moses Stuart, of Andover, and Lyman Beecher, of Connecticut. In the neighboring State of Connecticut, for example, there was until lately, for a period of several years, no distinctly Unitarian congregation worshiping in a church edifice of its own. On the other hand, the Unitarians claimed, with justice, that their opinions had to a great extent modified the theology of the orthodox churches. The writings of Horace Bushnell, of Hartford, one of the most eminent Congregational divines, approach Unitarianism in their interpretation of the doctrine of the Atonement; and the "progressive orthodoxy" of Andover is certainly not the Calvinism of Thomas Hooker or of Jonathan Edwards. But it seemed to the transcendentalists that conservative Unitarianism was too negative and "cultured," and Margaret Fuller complained of the coldness of the Boston pulpits. While contrariwise the central thought of transcendentalism, that the soul has an immediate connection with God, was pronounced by Dr. Channing a "crude speculation." This was the thought of Emerson's address in 1838 before the Cambridge Divinity School, and it was at once made the object of attack by conservative Unitarians like Henry Ware and Andrews Norton. The latter in an address before the same audience, on the *Latest Form of Infidelity*, said: "Nothing is left that can be called Christianity if its miraculous character be denied. . . . There can be no intuition, no direct perception of the truth of Christianity." And in a pamphlet supporting the same side of the question he added: "It is not an intelligible error but a mere absurdity to maintain that we are conscious, or have an intuitive knowledge, of the being of God, of our own immortality . . . or of any other fact of religion." Ripley and Parker replied in Emerson's defense; but Emerson himself would never be drawn into controversy. He said that he could not argue. He *announced* truths; his method was that of the seer, not of the disputant. In 1832 Emerson, who was a Unitarian clergyman, and descended from eight generations of clergymen, had resigned the pastorate of the Second Church of Boston because he could not conscientiously administer the sacrament of the communion—which he regarded as a mere act of commemoration—in the sense in which it was understood by his parishioners. Thenceforth, though he sometimes occupied Unitarian pulpits, and was, indeed, all his life a kind of "lay preacher," he never assumed the pastorate of a church. The representative of transcendentalism in the pulpit was Theodore Parker, an eloquent preacher, an eager debater and a prolific writer on many subjects, whose collected works fill fourteen volumes. Parker was a man of strongly human traits, passionate, independent, intensely religious, but intensely radical, who made for himself a large personal following. The more advanced wing of the Unitarians were called, after him, "Parkerites." Many of the Unitarian churches refused to "fellowship" with him; and the large congregation, or audience, which assembled in Music Hall to hear his sermons was stigmatized as a "boisterous assembly" which came to hear Parker preach irreligion.

It has been said that, on its philosophical side, New England transcendentalism was a restatement of idealism. The impulse came from Germany, from the philosophical writings of Kant, Fichte, Jacobi, and Schelling, and from the works of Coleridge and Carlyle, who had domesticated German thought in England. In Channing's *Remarks on a National Literature*, quoted in our last chapter, the essayist urged that our scholars should study the authors of France and Germany as one means of emancipating American letters from a slavish dependence on British literature. And in fact German literature began, not long after, to be eagerly studied in New England. Emerson published an American edition of Carlyle's *Miscellanies*, including his essays on German writers that had appeared in England between 1822 and 1830. In 1838 Ripley began to publish *Specimens of Foreign Standard Literature*, which extended to fourteen volumes. In his work of translating and supplying introductions to the matter selected he was helped by Ripley, Margaret Fuller, John S. Dwight and others who had more or less connection with the transcendental movement.

The definition of the new faith given by Emerson in his lecture on the *Transcendentalist*, 1842, is as follows: "What is popularly called transcendentalism among us is idealism. . . . The idealism of the present day acquired the name of transcendental from the use of that term by Immanuel Kant, who replied to the skeptical philosophy of Locke, which insisted that there was nothing in the intellect which was not previously in the experience of the senses, by showing that there was a very important class of ideas, or imperative forms, which did not come by experience, but through which experience was acquired; that these were intuitions of the mind itself, and he denominated them *transcendental* forms." Idealism denies the independent existence of matter. Transcendentalism claims for the innate ideas of God and the soul a higher assurance of reality than for the knowledge of the outside world derived through the senses. Emerson shares the "noble doubt" of idealism. He calls the universe a shade, a dream, "this great apparition." "It is a sufficient account of that appearance we call the world," he wrote in *Nature*, "that God will teach a human mind, and so makes it the receiver of a certain number of congruent sensations which we call sun and moon, man and woman, house and trade. In my utter impotence to test the authenticity of the report of my senses, to know whether the impressions on me correspond with outlying objects, what difference does it make whether Orion is up there in heaven or some god paints the image in the firmament of the soul?" On the other hand our evidence of the existence of God and of our own souls, and our knowledge of right and wrong, are immediate, and are independent of the senses.

We are in direct communication with the "Oversoul," the infinite Spirit. "The soul in man is the background of our being—an immensity not possessed, that cannot be possessed." "From within or from behind a light shines through us upon things, and makes us aware that we are nothing, but the light is all." Revelation is "an influx of the Divine mind into our mind. It is an ebb of the individual rivulet before the flowing surges of the sea of life." In moods of exaltation, and especially in the presence of nature, this contact of the individual soul with the absolute is felt. "All mean egotism vanishes. I become a transparent eyeball; I am nothing; I see all; the currents of the Universal Being circulate through me; I am part and particle of God." The existence and attributes of God are not deducible from history or from natural theology, but are thus directly given us in consciousness. In his essay on the *Transcendentalist*, Emerson says: "His experience inclines him to behold the procession of facts you call the world as flowing perpetually outward from an invisible, unsounded center in himself; center alike of him and of them and necessitating him to regard all things as having a subjective or relative existence — relative to that aforesaid Unknown Center of him. There is no bar or wall in the soul where man, the effect, ceases, and God, the cause, begins. We lie open on one side to the deeps of spiritual nature, to the attributes of God."

Emerson's point of view, though familiar to students of philosophy, is strange to the popular understanding, and hence has arisen the complaint of his obscurity. Moreover, he apprehended and expressed these ideas as a poet, in figurative and emotional language, and not as a metaphysician, in a formulated statement. His own position in relation to systematic philosophers is described in what he says of Plato, in his series of sketches entitled *Representative Men*, 1850: "He has not a system. The dearest disciples and defenders are at fault. He attempted a theory of the universe, and his theory is not complete or self-evident. One man thinks he means this, and another that; he has said one thing in one place, and the reverse of it in another place." It happens, therefore, that, to many students of more formal philosophies Emerson's meaning seems elusive, and he appears to write from temporary moods and to contradict himself. Had he attempted a reasoned exposition of the transcendental philosophy, instead of writing essays and poems, he might have added one more to the number of system-mongers; but he would not have taken that significant place which he occupies in the general literature of the time, nor exerted that wide influence upon younger writers which has been one of the stimulating forces in American thought. It was because Emerson was a poet that he is our Emerson. And yet it would be impossible to disentangle his peculiar philosophical ideas from the body of his writings and to leave the latter to stand upon their merits as literature merely. He is the poet of certain high abstractions, and his religion is central to all his work—excepting, perhaps, his *English Traits*, 1856, an acute study of national characteristics, and a few of his essays and verses, which are independent of any particular philosophical standpoint.

When Emerson resigned his parish in 1832 he made a short trip to Europe, where he visited Carlyle at Craigenputtoch, and Landor at Florence. On his return he retired to his birthplace, the village of Concord, Massachusetts, and settled down among his books and his fields, becoming a sort of "glorified farmer," but issuing frequently from his retirement to instruct and delight audiences of thoughtful people at Boston and at other points all through the country. Emerson was the perfection of a lyceum lecturer. His manner was quiet but forcible, his voice of charming quality, and his enunciation clean cut and refined. The sentence was his unit in composition. His lectures seemed to begin anywhere and to end anywhere, and to resemble strings of exquisitely polished sayings rather than continuous discourses. His printed essays, with unimportant exceptions, were first written and delivered as lectures. In 1836 he published his first book, *Nature*, which remains the most systematic statement of his philosophy. It opened a fresh spring-head in American thought, and the words of its introduction announced that its author had broken with the past. "Why should not we also enjoy an original relation to the universe? Why should not we have a poetry and philosophy of insight and not of tradition, and a religion by revelation to us and not the history of theirs?"

It took eleven years to sell five hundred copies of this little book. But the year following its publication the remarkable Phi Beta Kappa address at Cambridge, on the *American Scholar*, electrified the little public of the university. This is described by Lowell as "an event without any former parallel in our literary annals, a scene to be always treasured in the memory for its picturesqueness and its inspiration. What crowded and breathless aisles, what windows clustering with eager heads, what grim silence of foregone dissent!" To Concord came many kindred spirits, drawn by Emerson's magnetic attraction. Thither came, from Connecticut, Amos Bronson Alcott, born a few years before Emerson, whom he outlived; a quaint and benignant figure, a visionary and a mystic even among the trascendentalists themselves, and one who lived in unworldly simplicity the life of the soul. Alcott had taught school at Cheshire, Conn., and afterward at Boston on an original plan—compelling his scholars, for example, to flog *him*, when they did wrong, instead of taking a flogging themselves. The experiment was successful until his *Conversations on the Gospels*, in Boston, and his insistence upon admitting colored children to his benches, offended conservative opinion and broke up his school. Alcott renounced the eating of animal food in 1835. He believed in the union of thought and manual labor, and supported himself for some years by the work of his hands, gardening, cutting wood, etc. He traveled into the West and elsewhere, holding conversations on philosophy, education, and religion. He set up a little community at the village of Harvard, which was rather less successful than Brook Farm, and he contributed *Orphic Sayings* to the *Dial*, which were harder for the exoteric to understand than even Emerson's *Brahma* or the *Over-soul*.

Thither came, also, Sarah Margaret Fuller, the most intellectual woman of her time in America, an eager student of Greek and German literature and an ardent seeker after the True, the Good, and the Beautiful. She threw herself into many causes—temperance, antislavery, and the higher education of women. Her brilliant conversation classes in Boston attracted many "minds" of her own sex. Subsequently, as literary editor of the *New York Tribune*, she furnished a wider public with reviews and book-notices of great ability. She took part in the Brook Farm experiment, and she edited the *Dial* for a time, contributing to it the papers afterward expanded into her most considerable book, *Woman in the Nineteenth Century*. In 1846 she went abroad, and at Rome took part in the revolutionary movement of Mazzini, having charge of one of the hospitals during the siege of the city by the

French. In 1847 she married an impecunious Italian nobleman, the Marquis Ossoli. In 1850 the ship on which she was returning to America, with her husband and child, was wrecked on Fire Island beach and all three were lost. Margaret Fuller's collected writings are somewhat disappointing, being mainly of temporary interest. She lives less through her books than through the memoirs of her friends, Emerson, James Freeman Clarke, T. W. Higginson, and others who knew her as a personal influence. Her strenuous and rather overbearing individuality made an impression not altogether agreeable upon many of her contemporaries. Lowell introduced a caricature of her as "Miranda" into his *Fable for Critics*, and Hawthorne's caustic sketch of her, preserved in the biography written by his son, has given great offense to her admirers. "Such a determination to *eat* this huge universe!" was Carlyle's characteristic comment on her appetite for knowledge and aspirations after perfection.

To Concord also came Nathaniel Hawthorne, who took up his residence there first at the "Old Manse," and afterward at "The Wayside." Though naturally an idealist, he said that he came too late to Concord to fall decidedly under Emerson's influence. Of that he would have stood in little danger even had he come earlier. He appreciated the deep and subtle quality of Emerson's imagination, but his own shy genius always jealously guarded its independence and resented the too close approaches of an alien mind. Among the native disciples of Emerson at Concord the most noteworthy were Henry Thoreau, and his friend and biographer, William Ellery Channing, Jr., a nephew of the great Channing. Channing was a contributor to the *Dial*, and he published a volume of poems which elicited a fiercely contemptuous review from Edgar Poe. Though disfigured by affectation and obscurity, many of Channing's verses were distinguished by true poetic feeling, and the last line of his little piece, *A Poet's Hope*,

"If my bark sink 'tis to another sea,"

has taken a permanent place in the literature of transcendentalism.

The private organ of the transcendentalists was the *Dial*, a quarterly magazine, published from 1840 to 1844, and edited by Emerson and Margaret Fuller. Among its contributors, besides those already mentioned, were Ripley, Thoreau, Parker, James Freeman Clarke, Charles A. Dana, John S. Dwight, C. P. Cranch, Charles Emerson and William H. Channing, another nephew of Dr. Channing. It contained, along with a good deal of rubbish, some of the best poetry and prose that have been published in America. The most lasting part of its contents were the contributions of Emerson and Thoreau. But even as a whole, it is so unique a way-mark in the history of our literature that all its four volumes—copies of which had become scarce—have been recently reprinted in answer to a demand certainly very unusual in the case of an extinct periodical.

From time to time Emerson collected and published his lectures under various titles. A first series of *Essays* came out in 1841, and a second in 1844; the *Conduct of Life* in 1860, *Society and Solitude* in 1870, *Letters and Social Aims*, in 1876, and the *Fortune of the Republic* in 1878. In 1847 he issued a volume of *Poems*, and 1865 *Mayday and Other Poems*. These writings, as a whole, were variations on a single theme, expansions and illustrations of the philosophy set forth in *Nature*, and his early addresses. They were strikingly original, rich in thought, filled with wisdom, with lofty morality and spiritual religion. Emerson, said Lowell, first "cut the cable that bound us to English thought and gave us a chance at the dangers and glories of blue water." Nevertheless, as it used to be the fashion to find an English analogue for every American writer, so that Cooper was called the American Scott, and Mrs. Sigourney was described as the Hemans of America, a well-worn critical tradition has coupled Emerson with Carlyle. That his mind received a nudge from Carlyle's early essays and from *Sartor Resartus* is beyond a doubt. They were life-long friends and correspondents, and Emerson's *Representative Men* is, in some sort, a counterpart of Carlyle's *Hero Worship*. But in temper and style the two writers were widely different. Carlyle's pessimism and dissatisfaction with the general drift of things gained upon him more and more, while Emerson was a consistent optimist to the end. The last of his writings published during his life-time, the *Fortune of the Republic*, contrasts strangely in its hopefulness with the desperation of Carlyle's later utterances. Even in presence of the doubt as to man's personal immortality he takes refuge in a high and stoical faith. "I think all sound minds rest on a certain preliminary conviction, namely: that if it be best that conscious personal life shall continue it will continue, and if not best, then it will not; and we, if we saw the whole, should of course see that it was better so." It is this conviction that gives to Emerson's writings their serenity and their tonic quality at the same time that it narrows the range of his dealings with life. As the idealist declines to cross-examine those facts which he regards as merely phenomenal, and looks upon this outward face of things as upon a mask not worthy to dismay the fixed soul, so the optimist turns away his eyes from the evil which he disposes of as merely negative, as the shadow of the good. Hawthorne's interest in the problem of sin finds little place in Emerson's philosophy. Passion comes not nigh him and *Faust* disturbs him with its disagreeableness. Pessimism is to him "the only skepticism."

The greatest literature is that which is most broadly human, or, in other words, that which will square best with all philosophies. But Emerson's genius was interpretive rather than constructive. The poet dwells in the cheerful world of phenomena. He is most the poet who realizes most intensely the good and the bad of human life. But Idealism makes experience shadowy and subordinates action to contemplation. To it the cities of men, with their "frivolous populations,".

> " . . . are but sailing foam-bells
> Along thought's causing stream."

Shakespere does not forget that the world will one day vanish "like the baseless fabric of a vision," and that we ourselves are "such stuff as dreams are made on;" but this is not the mood in which he dwells. Again: while it is for the philosopher to reduce variety to unity, it is the poet's task to detect the manifold under uniformity. In the great creative poets, in Shakespere and Dante and Goethe, how infinite the swarm of persons, the multitude of forms! But with Emerson the type is important, the common element. "In youth we are mad for persons. But the larger experience of man discovers the identical nature appearing through them all." "The same—the same!" he exclaims in his essay on *Plato*. "Friend and foe are of one stuff; the plowman, the plow and the furrow are of one stuff." And this is the thought in *Brahma*:

> "They reckon ill who leave me out;
> When me they fly I am the wings:
> I am the doubter and the doubt,
> And I the hymn the Brahmin sings."

It is not easy to fancy a writer who holds this altitude toward "persons" descending to the composition of a novel or a play. Emerson showed, indeed, a fine power of character analysis in his *English Traits* and *Representative Men* and in his memoirs of Thoreau and Margaret Fuller. There is even a sort of dramatic humor in his portrait of Socrates. But upon the whole he stands midway between constructive artists, whose instinct it is to tell a story or sing a song, and philosophers, like Schelling, who give poetic expression to a system of thought. He belongs to the class of minds of which Sir Thomas Browne is the best English example. He set a high value upon Browne, to whose style his own, though far more sententious, bears a resemblance. Browne's saying, for example, "All things are artificial, for nature is the art of God," sounds like Emerson, whose workmanship, for the rest, in his prose essays was exceedingly fine and close. He was not afraid to be homely and racy in expressing thought of the highest spirituality. "Hitch your wagon to a star" is a good instance of his favorite manner.

Emerson's verse often seems careless in technique. Most of his pieces are scrappy and have the air of runic rimes, or little oracular "voicings"—as they say in Concord—in rhythmic shape, of single thoughts on "Worship," "Character," "Heroism," "Art," "Politics," "Culture," etc. The content is the important thing, and the form is too frequently awkward or bald. Sometimes, indeed, in the clear-obscure of Emerson's poetry the deep wisdom of the thought finds its most natural expression in the imaginative simplicity of the language. But though this artlessness in him became too frequently in his imitators, like Thoreau and Ellery Channing, an obtruded simplicity, among his own poems are many that leave nothing to be desired in point of wording and of verse. His *Hymn Sung at the Completion of the Concord Monument*, in 1836, is the perfect model of an occasional poem. Its lines were on every one's lips at the time of the centennial celebrations in 1876, and "the shot heard round the world" has hardly echoed farther than the song which chronicled it. Equally current is the stanza from *Voluntaries:*

> "So nigh is grandeur to our dust,
> So near is God to man,
> When Duty whispers low, "Thou must,'
> The youth replies, 'I can.'"

So, too, the famous lines from the *Problem:*

> "The hand that rounded Peter's dome,
> And groined the aisles of Christian Rome,
> Wrought in a sad sincerity.
> Himself from God he could not free;
> He builded better than he knew;
> The conscious stone to beauty grew."

The most noteworthy of Emerson's pupils was Henry David Thoreau, "the poet-naturalist." After his graduation from Harvard College, in 1837, Thoreau engaged in school teaching and in the manufacture of lead-pencils, but soon gave up all regular business and devoted himself to walking, reading, and the study of nature. He was at one time private tutor in a family on Staten Island, and he supported himself for a season by doing odd jobs in land surveying for the farmers about Concord. In 1845 he built, with his own hands, a small cabin on the banks of Walden Pond, near Concord, and lived there in seclusion for two years. His expenses during these years were nine cents a day, and he gave an account of his experiment in his most characteristic book, *Walden*, published in 1854. His *Week on the Concord and Merrimac Rivers* appeared in 1849. From time to time he went farther afield, and his journeys were reported in *Cape Cod*, the *Maine Woods, Excursions*, and a *Yankee in Canada*, all of which, as well as a volume of *Letters* and *Early Spring in Massachusetts*, have been given to the public since his death, which happened in 1862. No one has lived so close to nature, and written of it so intimately, as Thoreau. His life was a lesson in economy and a sermon on Emerson's text, "Lessen your denominator." He wished to reduce existence to the simplest terms—to

> " live all alone
> Close to the bone,
> And where life is sweet
> Constantly eat."

He had a passion for the wild, and seems like an Anglo-Saxon reversion to the type of the Red

Indian. The most distinctive note in Thoreau is his inhumanity. Emerson spoke of him as a "perfect piece of stoicism." "Man," said Thoreau, "is only the point on which I stand." He strove to realize the objective life of nature—nature in its aloofness from man; to identify himself, with the moose and the mountain. He listened, with his ear close to the ground, for the voice of the earth. "What are the trees saying?" he exclaimed. Following upon the trail of the lumberman he asked the primeval wilderness for its secret, and

> "saw beneath dim aisles, in odorous beds,
> The slight linnæa hang its twin-born heads."

He tried to interpret the thought of Ktaadn and to fathom the meaning of the billows on the back of Cape Cod, in their indifference to the shipwrecked bodies that they rolled ashore. "After sitting in my chamber many days, reading the poets, I have been out early on a foggy morning and heard the cry of an owl in a neighboring wood as from a nature behind the common, unexplored by science or by literature. None of the feathered race has yet realized my youthful conceptions of the woodland depths. I had seen the red election-birds brought from their recesses on my comrade's string, and fancied that their plumage would assume stranger and more dazzling colors, like the tints of evening, in proportion as I advanced farther into the darkness and solitude of the forest. Still less have I seen such strong and wild tints on any poet's string."

It was on the mystical side that Thoreau apprehended transcendentalism. Mysticism has been defined as the soul's recognition of its identity with nature. This thought lies plainly in Schelling's philosophy, and he illustrated it by his famous figure of the magnet. Mind and nature are one; they are the positive and negative poles of the magnet. In man, the Absolute—that is, God—becomes conscious of himself; makes of himself, as nature, an object to himself as mind. "The souls of men," said Schelling, "are but the innumerable individual eyes with which our infinite World-Spirit beholds himself." This thought is also clearly present in Emerson's view of nature, and has caused him to be accused of pantheism. But if by pantheism is meant the doctrine that the underlying principle of the universe is matter or force, none of the transcendentalists was a pantheist. In their view nature was divine. Their poetry is always haunted by the sense of a spiritual reality which abides beyond the phenomena. Thus in Emerson's *Two Rivers:*

> "Thy summer voice, Musketaquit,*
> Repeats the music of the rain,
> But sweeter rivers pulsing flit
>   Through thee as thou through Concord plain.
>
> "Thou in thy narrow banks art pent:
> The stream I love unbounded goes;
> Through flood and sea and firmament,
>   Through light, through life, it forward flows.

---

* The Indian name of Concord River.

"I see the inundation sweet,
  I hear the spending of the stream,
Through years, through men, through nature fleet,
  Through passion, thought, through power and dream."

This mood occurs frequently in Thoreau. The hard world of matter becomes suddenly all fluent and spiritual, and he sees himself in it—sees God. "This earth," he cries, "which is spread out like a map around me, is but the lining of my inmost soul exposed." "In *me* is the sucker that I see;" and, of Walden Pond,

"I am its stony shore,
And the breeze that passes o'er."

"Suddenly old Time winked at me—ah, you know me, you rogue—and news had come that IT was well. That ancient universe is in such capital health, I think, undoubtedly, it will never die.... I see, smell, taste, hear, feel that everlasting something to which we are allied, at once our maker, our abode, our destiny, our very selves." It was something ulterior that Thoreau sought in nature. "The other world," he wrote, "is all my art: my pencils will draw no other: my jack-knife will cut nothing else." Thoreau did not scorn, however, like Emerson, to "examine too microscopically the universal tablet." He was a close observer and accurate reporter of the ways of birds and plants and the minuter aspects of nature. He has had many followers, who have produced much pleasant literature on out-door life. But in none of them is there that unique combination of the poet, the naturalist and the mystic which gives his page its wild original flavor. He had the woodcraft of a hunter and the eye of a botanist, but his imagination did not stop short with the fact. The sound of a tree falling in the Maine woods was to him "as though a door had shut somewhere in the damp and shaggy wilderness." He saw small things in cosmic relations. His trip down the tame Concord has for the reader the excitement of a voyage of exploration into far and unknown regions. The river just above Sherman's Bridge, in time of flood "when the wind blows freshly on a raw March day, heaving up the surface into dark and sober billows," was like Lake Huron, "and you may run aground on Cranberry Island," and "get as good a freezing there as anywhere on the North-west coast." He said that most of the phenomena described in Kane's voyages could be observed in Concord.

The literature of transcendentalism was like the light of the stars in a winter night, keen and cold and high. It had the pale cast of thought, and was almost too spiritual and remote to "hit the sense of mortal sight." But it was at least indigenous. If not an American literature—not national and not inclusive of all sides of American life—it was, at all events, a genuine New England literature and true to the spirit of its section. The tough Puritan stock had at last put forth a blossom which compared with the warm, robust growths of English soil even as the delicate wind flower of the northern spring compares with the cowslips and daisies of old England.

In 1842 Nathaniel Hawthorne (1804-1864) the greatest American romancer, came to Concord. He had recently left Brook Farm, had just been married, and with his bride he settled down in the "Old Manse" for three paradisaical years. A picture of this protracted honeymoon and this sequestered life, as tranquil as the slow stream on whose banks it was passed, is given in the introductory chapter to his *Mosses from an Old Manse*, 1846, and in the more personal and confidential records of his *American Note Books*, posthumously published. Hawthorne was thirty-eight when he took his place among the Concord literati. His childhood and youth had been spent partly at his birthplace, the old and already somewhat decayed sea-port town of Salem, and partly at his grandfather's farm on Sebago Lake, in Maine, then on the edge of the primitive forest. Maine did not become a State, indeed, until 1820, the year before Hawthorne entered Bowdoin College, whence he was graduated in 1825, in the same class with Henry W. Longfellow and one year behind Franklin Pierce, afterward President of the United States. After leaving college Hawthorne buried himself for years in the seclusion of his home at Salem. His mother, who was early widowed, had withdrawn entirely from the world. For months at a time Hawthorne kept his room, seeing no other society than that of his mother and sisters, reading all sorts of books and writing wild tales, most of which he destroyed as soon as he had written them. At twilight he would emerge from the house for a solitary ramble through the streets of the town or along the sea-side. Old Salem had much that was picturesque in its associations. It had been the scene of the witch trials in the seventeenth century, and it abounded in ancient mansions, the homes of retired whalers and India merchants. Hawthorne's father had been a ship captain, and many of his ancestors had followed the sea. One of his forefathers, moreover, had been a certain Judge Hawthorne, who in 1691 had sentenced several of the witches to death. The thought of this affected Hawthorne's imagination with a pleasing horror and he utilized it afterward in his *House of the Seven Gables.* Many of the old Salem houses, too, had their family histories, with now and then the hint of some obscure crime or dark misfortune which haunted posterity with its curse till all the stock died out, or fell into poverty and evil ways, as in the Pyncheon family of Hawthorne's romance. In the preface to the *Marble Faun* Hawthorne wrote: "No author without a trial can conceive of the difficulty of writing a romance about a country where there is no shadow, no antiquity, no mystery, no picturesque and gloomy wrong, nor any thing but a commonplace prosperity in broad and simple daylight." And yet it may be doubted whether any environment could have been found more fitted to his peculiar genius than this of his native town, or any preparation better calculated to ripen the faculty that was in him than these long, lonely years of waiting and brooding thought. From time to time he contributed a story or a sketch to some periodical, such as S. G. Goodrich's Annual, the *Token*, or the *Knickerbocker Magazine*. Some of these attracted the attention of the judicious; but they were anonymous and signed by various *noms de plume*, and their author was at this time—to use his own words—"the obscurest man of letters in America." In 1828 he had issued anonymously and at his own expense a short romance, entitled *Fanshawe*. It had little success, and copies of the first edition are now exceedingly rare. In 1837 he published a collection of his magazine pieces under the title, *Twice Told Tales*. The book was generously praised in the *North American Review* by his former classmate, Longfellow; and Edgar Poe showed his keen critical perception by predicting that the writer would easily put himself at the head of imaginative literature in America if he would discard allegory, drop short stories and compose a genuine romance. Poe compared Hawthorne's work with that of the German romancer, Tieck, and it is interesting to find confirmation of this dictum in passages of the *American Note Books*, in which Hawthorne speaks of laboring over Tieck with a German dictionary. The

Twice Told Tales are the work of a recluse, who makes guesses at life from a knowledge of his own heart, acquired by a habit of introspection, but who has had little contact with men. Many of them were shadowy and others were morbid and unwholesome. But their gloom was of an interior kind, never the physically horrible of Poe. It arose from weird psychological situations like that of *Ethan Brand* in his search for the unpardonable sin. Hawthorne was true to the inherited instinct of Puritanism; he took the conscience for his theme, and in these early tales he was already absorbed in the problem of evil, the subtle ways in which sin works out its retribution, and the species of fate or necessity that the wrong-doer makes for himself in the inevitable sequences of his crime. Hawthorne was strongly drawn toward symbols and types, and never quite followed Poe's advice to abandon allegory. The *Scarlet Letter* and his other romances are not, indeed, strictly allegories, since the characters are men and women and not mere personifications of abstract qualities. Still they all have a certain allegorical tinge. In the *Marble Faun*, for example, Hilda, Kenyon, Miriam and Donatello have been ingeniously explained as personifications respectively of the conscience, the reason, the imagination and the senses. Without going so far as this, it is possible to see in these and in Hawthorne's other creations something typical and representative. He uses his characters like algebraic symbols to work out certain problems with: they are rather more and yet rather less than flesh and blood individuals. The stories in *Twice Told Tales* and in the second collection, *Mosses from an Old Manse*, 1846, are more openly allegorical than his later work. Thus the *Minister's Black Veil* is a sort of anticipation of Arthur Dimmesdale in the *Scarlet Letter*. From 1846 to 1849 Hawthorne held the position of Surveyor of the Custom House of Salem. In the preface to the *Scarlet Letter* he sketched some of the government officials with whom this office had brought him into contact in a way that gave some offense to the friends of the victims and a great deal of amusement to the public. Hawthorne's humor was quiet and fine, like Irving's, but less genial and with a more satiric edge to it. The book last named was written at Salem and published in 1850, just before its author's removal to Lenox, now a sort of inland Newport, but then an unfashionable resort among the Berkshire hills. Whatever obscurity may have hung over Hawthorne hitherto was effectually dissolved by this powerful tale, which was as vivid in coloring as the implication of its title. Hawthorne chose for his background the somber life of the early settlers in New England. He had always been drawn toward this part of American history, and in *Twice Told Tales* had given some illustrations of it in *Endicott's Red Cross* and *Legends of the Province House*. Against this dark foil moved in strong relief the figures of Hester

Prynne, the woman taken in adultery, her paramour, the Rev. Arthur Dimmesdale, her husband, old Roger Chillingworth, and her illegitimate child. In tragic power, in its grasp of the elementary passions of human nature and its deep and subtle insight into the inmost secrets of the heart, this is Hawthorne's greatest book. He never crowded his canvas with figures. In the *Blithedale Romance* and the *Marble Faun* there is the same *parti carré* or group of four characters. In the *House of the Seven Gables* there are five. The last mentioned of these, published in 1852, was of a more subdued intensity than the *Scarlet Letter*, but equally original and, upon the whole, perhaps equally good. The *Blithedale Romance*, published in the same year, though not strikingly inferior to the others, adhered more to conventional patterns in its plot and in the sensational nature of its ending. The suicide of the heroine by drowning, and the terrible scene of the recovery of her body, were suggested to the author by an experience of his own on Concord River, the account of which, in his own words, may be read in Julian Hawthorne's *Nathaniel Hawthorne and His Wife*. In 1852 Hawthorne returned to Concord and bought the "Wayside" property, which he retained until his death. But in the following year his old college friend Pierce, now become President, appointed him Consul to Liverpool, and he went abroad for seven years. The most valuable fruit of his foreign residence was the romance of the *Marble Faun*, 1860; the longest of his fictions and the richest in descriptive beauty. The theme of this was the development of the soul through the experience of sin. There is a haunting mystery thrown about the story, like a soft veil of mist, veiling the beginning and the end. There is even a delicate teasing suggestion of the preternatural in Donatello, the Faun, a creation as original as Shakspere's Caliban, or Fouqué's Undine, and yet quite on this side the border-line of the human. *Our Old Home*, a book of charming papers on England, was published in 1863. Manifold experience of life and contact with men, affording scope for his always keen observation, had added range, fullness, warmth to the imaginative subtlety which had manifested itself even in his earliest tales. Two admirable books for children, the *Wonder Book* and *Tanglewood Tales*, in which the classical mythologies were retold, should also be mentioned in the list of Hawthorne's writings, as well as the *American*, *English*, and *Italian Note Books*, the first of which contains the seed thoughts of some of his finished works, together with hundreds of hints for plots, episodes, descriptions, etc., which he never found time to work out. Hawthorne's style, in his first sketches and stories a little stilted and "bookish," gradually acquired an exquisite perfection, and is as well worth study as that of any prose classic in the English tongue.

Hawthorne was no transcendentalist. He dwelt

much in a world of ideas, and he sometimes doubted whether the tree on the bank or its image in the stream were the more real. But this had little in common with the philosophical idealism of his neighbors. He reverenced Emerson, and he held kindly intercourse—albeit a silent man and easily bored—with Thoreau and Ellery Channing, and even with Margaret Fuller. But his sharp eyes saw whatever was whimsical or weak in the apostles of the new faith. He had little enthusiasm for causes or reforms, and among so many Abolitionists he remained a Democrat, and even wrote a campaign life of his friend Pierce.

The village of Concord has perhaps done more for American literature than the city of New York. Certainly there are few places where associations, both patriotic and poetic, cluster so thickly. At one side of the grounds of the Old Manse—which has the river at its back—runs down a shaded lane to the Concord monument and the figure of the Minute Man and the successor of "the rude bridge that arched the flood." Scarce two miles away, among the woods, is little Walden—"God's drop." The men who made Concord famous are asleep in Sleepy Hollow, yet still their memory prevails to draw seekers after truth to the Concord Summer School of Philosophy, which meets every year, to reason high of "God, Freedom, and Immortality," next-door to the "Wayside," and under the hill on whose ridge Hawthorne wore a path, as he paced up and down beneath the hemlocks.

1 Ralph Waldo Emerson. Nature. The American Scholar. Literary Ethics. The Transcendentalist. The Over-soul. Address before the Cambridge Divinity School. English Traits. Representative Men. Poems.

2. Henry David Thoreau. Excursions. Walden. A Week on the Concord and Merrimac Rivers. Cape Cod. The Maine Woods.

3. Nathaniel Hawthorne. Mosses from an Old Manse. The Scarlet Letter. The House of the Seven Gables. The Blithedale Romance. The Marble Faun. Our Old Home.

4. Transcendentalism in New England. By O. B. Frothingham. New York: G. P. Putnam's Sons. 1875.

CHAPTER V.

THE CAMBRIDGE SCHOLARS.

1837-1861.

WITH few exceptions, the men who have made American literature what it is have been college graduates. And yet our colleges have not commonly been, in themselves, literary centers. Most of them have been small and poor, and situated in little towns or provincial cities. Their alumni scatter far and wide immediately after graduation, and even those of them who may feel drawn to a life of scholarship or letters find little to attract them at the home of their *alma mater*, and seek, by preference, the large cities where periodicals and publishing houses offer some hope of support in a literary career. Even in the older and better equipped universities the faculty is usually a corps of working scholars, each man intent upon his specialty and rather inclined to undervalue merely "literary" performance. In many cases the fastidious and hypercritical turn of mind which besets the scholar, the timid conservatism which naturally characterizes an ancient seat of learning and the spirit of theological conformity which suppresses free discussion have exerted their benumbing influence upon the originality and creative impulse of their inmates. Hence it happens that, while the contributions of American college teachers to the exact sciences, to theology and philology, metaphysics, political philosophy and the severer branches of learning have been honorable and important, they have as a class made little mark upon the general literature of the country. The professors of literature in our colleges are usually persons who have made no additions to literature, and the professors of rhetoric seem ordinarily to have been selected to teach students how to write, for the reason that they themselves have never written any thing that any one has ever read.

To these remarks the Harvard College of some fifty years ago offers a striking exception. It was not the large and fashionable university that it has lately grown to be, with its multiplied elective courses, its numerous faculty and its somewhat motley collection of undergraduates; but a small school of the classics and mathematics, with something of ethics, natural science and the modern languages added to its old-fashioned, scholastic curriculum, and with a very homogeneous *clientèle*, drawn mainly from the Unitarian families of Eastern Massachusetts. Nevertheless a finer intellectual life, in many respects, was lived at old Cambridge within the years covered by this chapter than nowadays at the same place, or at any date in any other American university town. The neighborhood of Boston, where the commercial life has never so entirely overlain the intellectual as in New York and Philadelphia, has been a standing advantage to Harvard College. The recent upheaval in religious thought had secured toleration, and made possible that free and even audacious interchange of ideas without which a literary atmosphere is impossible. From these, or from whatever causes, it happened that the old Harvard scholarship had an elegant and tasteful side to it, so that the dry erudition of the schools blossomed into a generous culture, and there were men in the professors' chairs who were no less efficient as teachers because they were also poets, orators, wits and men of the world. In the seventeen years from 1821 to 1839 there were graduated from Harvard College Emerson, Holmes, Sumner, Phillips, Motley, Thoreau, Lowell, and Edward Everett Hale, some of whom took up their residence at Cambridge, others at Boston and others at Concord, which was quite as much a spiritual suburb of Boston as Cambridge was. In 1836, when Longfellow became Professor of Modern Languages at Harvard, Sumner was lecturing in the Law School. The following year— in which Thoreau took his bachelor's degree— witnessed the delivery of Emerson's Phi Beta Kappa lecture on the *American Scholar* in the college chapel and Wendell Phillips's speech on the *Murder of Lovejoy* in Faneuil Hall. Lowell, whose description of the impression produced by the former of these famous addresses has been quoted in a previous chapter, was an undergraduate at the time. He took his degree in 1838 and in 1855 succeeded Longfellow in the chair of Modern Languages. Holmes had been chosen in 1847 Professor of Anatomy and Philosophy in the Medical School—a position which he held until 1882. The historians, Prescott and Bancroft, had been graduated in 1814 and 1817 respectively. The former's first important publication, *Ferdinand and Isabella*, appeared in 1837. Bancroft had been a tutor in the college in 1822–23 and the initial volume of his *History of the United States* was issued in 1835. Another of the Massachusetts school of historical writers, Francis Parkman, took his first degree at Harvard in 1844. Cambridge was still hardly more than a village, a rural outskirt of Boston, such as Lowell described it in his article, *Cambridge Thirty Years Ago*, originally contributed to *Putnam's Monthly* in 1853, and afterward reprinted in his *Fireside Travels*, 1864. The situation of a university scholar in old Cambridge was thus an almost ideal one. Within easy reach of a great city, with its literary and social clubs, its theaters, lecture courses, public meetings, dinner parties, etc., he yet lived withdrawn in an academic retirement among elm-shaded avenues and leafy gardens, the dome of the Boston State-house looming distantly across the meadows where the Charles laid its "steel blue sickle" upon the variegated, plush-like ground of the wide marsh. There was thus, at all times during the quarter of a century embraced between 1837 and 1861, a group of brilliant men resident in or about Cambridge and Boston, meeting frequently and intimately, and exerting upon one another a most stimulating influence. Some of the closer circles—all concentric to the university—of which this group was loosely composed were laughed at by outsiders as "Mutual Admiration Societies." Such was, for instance, the "Five of Clubs," whose members were Longfellow, Sumner, C. C. Felton, Professor of Greek at Harvard, and afterward president of the college; G. S. Hillard, a graceful lecturer, essayist and poet, of a somewhat amateurish kind; and Henry R. Cleveland, of Jamaica Plain, a lover of books and a writer of them.

Henry Wadsworth Longfellow (1807-1882) the most widely read and loved of American poets—or indeed, of all contemporary poets in England and America—though identified with Cambridge for nearly fifty years was a native of Portland, Maine, and a graduate of Bowdoin College, in the same class with Hawthorne. Since leaving college, in 1825, he had studied and traveled for some years in Europe, and had held the professorship of modern languages at Bowdoin. He had published several text books, a number of articles on the Romance languages and literatures in the *North American Review*, a thin volume of metrical translations from the Spanish, a few original poems in various periodicals, and the pleasant sketches of European travel entitled *Outre Mer*. But Longfellow's fame began with the appearance in 1839 of his *Voices of the Night*. Excepting an earlier collection by Bryant this was the first volume of real poetry published in New England, and it had more warmth and sweetness, a greater richness and variety than Bryant's work ever possessed. Longfellow's genius was almost feminine in its flexibility and its sympathetic quality. It readily took the color of its surroundings and opened itself eagerly to impressions of the beautiful from every quarter, but especially from books. This first volume contained a few things written during his student days at Bowdoin, one of which, a blank verse piece on *Autumn*, clearly shows the influence of Bryant's *Thanatopsis*. Most of these *juvenilia* had nature for their theme, but they were not so sternly true to the New England landscape as Thoreau or Bryant. The skylark and the ivy appear among their scenic properties, and in the best of them, *Woods in Winter*, it is the English "hawthorn" and not any American tree, through which the gale is made to blow, just as later Longfellow uses "rooks" instead of crows. The young poet's fancy was instinctively putting out feelers toward the storied lands of the Old World, and in his *Hymn of the Moravian Nuns of Bethlehem* he transformed the rude church of the Moravian sisters to a cathedral with "glimmering tapers," swinging censers, chancel, altar, cowls and "dim mysterious aisle." After his visit to Europe, Longfellow returned deeply imbued with the spirit of romance. It was his mission to refine our national taste by opening to American readers, in their own vernacular, new springs of beauty in the literatures of foreign tongues. The fact that this mission was interpretative, rather than creative, hardly detracts from Longfellow's true originality. It merely indicates that his inspiration came to him in the first instance from other sources than the common life about him. He naturally began as a translator, and this first volume contained, among other things, exquisite renderings from the German of Uhland, Salis, and Müller, from the Danish, French, Spanish and Anglo-Saxon, and a few passages from Dante. Longfellow remained all his life a translator, and in subtler ways than by direct translation he infused the fine essence of European poetry into his own. He loved—

"Tales that have the rime of age
And chronicles of eld."

The golden light of romance is shed upon his page, and it is his habit to borrow mediæval and Catholic imagery from his favorite middle ages, even when writing of American subjects. To him the clouds are hooded friars, that "tell their beads in drops of rain;" the midnight winds blowing through woods and mountain passes are chanting solemn masses for the repose of the dying year, and the strain ends with the prayer—

"Kyrie, eleyson,
Christe, eleyson."

In his journal he wrote characteristically: "The black shadows lie upon the grass like engravings in a book. Autumn has written his rubric on the illuminated leaves, the wind turns them over and chants like a friar." This in Cambridge, of a moonshiny night, on the first day of the American October. But several of the pieces in *Voices of the Night* sprang more immediately from the poet's own inner experience. The *Hymn to the Night*, the *Psalm of Life*, the *Reaper and the Flowers*, *Footsteps of Angels*, the *Light of Stars*, and the *Beleaguered City* spoke of love, bereavement, comfort, patience and faith. In these lovely songs and in many others of the same kind which he afterward wrote, Longfellow touched the hearts of all his countrymen. America is a country of homes, and Longfellow, as the poet of sentiment and of the domestic affections, became and remains far more general in his appeal than such a "cosmic" singer as Whitman, who is still practically unknown to the "fierce democracy" to which he has addressed himself. It would be hard to overestimate the influence for good exerted by the tender feeling and the pure and sweet morality which the hundreds of thousands of copies of Longfellow's writings, that have been circulated among readers of all classes in America and England, have brought with them.

Three later collections, *Ballads and Other Poems*, 1842; the *Belfry of Bruges*, 1846; and the *Seaside and the Fireside*, 1850, comprise most of what is noteworthy in Longfellow's minor poetry. The first of these embraced, together with some renderings from the German and the Scandinavian languages, specimens of stronger original work than the author had yet put forth; namely, the two powerful ballads of the *Skeleton in Armor* and the *Wreck of the Hesperus*. The former of these, written in the swift leaping meter of Drayton's *Ode to the Cambro Britons on their Harp*, was suggested by the digging up of a mail-clad skeleton at Fall River—a circumstance which the poet linked with the traditions about the Round Tower at Newport and gave to the whole the spirit of a Norse viking song of war and of the sea. The *Wreck of the Hesperus* was occasioned by the news of shipwrecks on the coast near Gloucester and by the name of a reef—" Norman's Woe "—where many of them took place. It was written one night between twelve and three, and cost the poet, he said, "hardly an effort." Indeed, it is the spontaneous ease and grace, the unfailing taste of Lonfellow's lines, which are their best technical quality. There is nothing obscure or esoteric about his poetry. If there is little passion or intellectual depth, there is always genuine poetic feeling, often a very high order of imagination and almost invariably the choice of the right word. In this volume were also included the *Village Blacksmith* and *Excelsior*. The latter, and the *Psalm of Life*, have had a " damnable iteration " which causes them to figure as Longfellow's most popular pieces. They are by no means, however, among his best. They are vigorously expressed commonplaces of that hortatory kind which passes for poetry, but is, in reality, a vague species of preaching.

In the *Belfry of Bruges* and the *Seaside and the Fireside*, the translations were still kept up, and among the original pieces were the *Occultation of Orion* — the most imaginative of all Longfellow's poems; *Seaweed*, which has very noble stanzas, the favorite *Old Clock on the Stairs*, the *Building of the Ship*, with its magnificent closing apostrophe to the Union, and the *Fire of Driftwood*, the subtlest in feeling of any thing that the poet ever wrote. With these were verses of a more familiar quality, such as the *Bridge*, *Resignation*, and the *Day Is Done*, and many others, all reflecting moods of gentle and pensive sentiment, and drawing from analogies in nature or in legend lessons which, if somewhat obvious, were expressed with perfect art. Like Keats, he apprehended every thing on its beautiful side. Longfellow was all poet. Like Ophelia in *Hamlet*,

"Thought and affection, passion, hell itself,
He turns to favor and to prettiness."

He cared very little about the intellectual movement of the age. The transcendental ideas of Emerson passed over his head and left him undisturbed. For politics he had that gentlemanly distaste which the cultivated class in America had already begun to entertain. In 1842 he printed a small volume of *Poems on Slavery*, which drew commendation from his friend Sumner, but had nothing of the fervor of Whittier's or Lowell's utterances on the same subject. It is interesting to compare his journals with Hawthorne's *American Note Books* and to observe in what very different ways the two writers made prey of their daily experiences for literary material. A favorite haunt of Longfellow's was the bridge between Boston and Cambridgeport, the same which he put into verse in his poem, the *Bridge*. "I always stop on the bridge," he writes in his journal; "tide waters are beautiful. From the ocean up into the land they go, like messengers, to ask why the tribute has not been paid. The brooks and rivers answer that there has been little harvest of snow and rain this year. Floating sea-weed and kelp is carried up into the meadows, as returning sailors bring oranges in bandanna handkerchiefs to friends in the country." And again: "We leaned for awhile on the wooden rail and enjoyed the silvery reflection on the sea, making sundry comparisons. Among other thoughts we had this cheering one, that the whole sea was flashing with this heavenly light, though we saw it only in a single track; the dark waves are the dark providences of God; luminous, though not to us; and even to ourselves in another position." "Walk on the bridge, both ends of which are lost in the fog, like human life midway between two eternities;

beginning and ending in mist." In Hawthorne an allegoric meaning is usually something deeper and subtler than this, and seldom so openly expressed. Many of Longfellow's poems—the *Beleaguered City*, for example—may be definitely divided into two parts; in the first, a story is told or a natural phenomenon described; in the second, the spiritual application of the parable is formally set forth. This method became with him almost a trick of style, and his readers learned to look for the *hæc fabula docet* at the end as a matter of course. As for the prevailing optimism in Longfellow's view of life—of which the above passage is an instance —it seemed to be in him an affair of temperament, and not, as in Emerson, the result of philosophic insight. Perhaps, however, in the last analysis optimism and pessimism are subjective—the expression of temperament or individual experience, since the facts of life are the same, whether seen through Schopenhauer's eyes or through Emerson's. If there is any particular in which Longfellow's inspiration came to him at first hand and not through books, it is in respect to the aspects of the sea. On this theme no American poet has written more beautifully and with a keener sympathy than the author of the *Wreck of the Hesperus* and of *Seaweed.*

In 1847 was published the long poem of *Evangeline*. The story of the Acadian peasant girl, who was separated from her lover in the dispersion of her people by the English troops, and after weary wanderings and a life-long search found him at last, an old man dying in a Philadelphia hospital, was told to Longfellow by the Rev. H. L. Conolly, who had previously suggested it to Hawthorne as a subject for a story. Longfellow, characteristically enough, "got up" the local color for his poem from Haliburton's account of the dispersion of the Grand-Pré Acadians, from Darby's *Geographical Description of Louisiana* and Watson's *Annals of Philadelphia*. He never needed to go much outside of his library for literary impulse and material. Whatever may be held as to Longfellow's inventive powers as a creator of characters or an interpreter of American life, his originality as an artist is manifested by his successful domestication in *Evangeline* of the dactylic hexameter, which no English poet had yet used with effect. The English poet, Arthur Hugh Clough, who lived for a time in Cambridge, followed Longfellow's example in the use of hexameter in his *Bothie of Tober-na-Vuolich*, so that we have now arrived at the time—a proud moment for American letters—when the works of our writers began to react upon the literature of Europe. But the beauty of the descriptions in *Evangeline* and the pathos—somewhat too drawn out—of the story made it dear to a multitude of readers who cared nothing about the technical disputes of Poe and other critics as to whether or not Longfellow's lines were sufficiently "spondaic" to truthfully represent the quantitative hexameters of Homer and Vergil.

In 1855 appeared *Hiawatha*, Longfellow's most

aboriginal and "American" book. The tripping trochaic measure he borrowed from the Finnish epic *Kalevala*. The vague, childlike mythology of the Indian tribes, with its anthropomorphic sense of the brotherhood between men, animals, and the forms of inanimate nature, he took from Schoolcraft's *Algic Researches*, 1839. He fixed forever, in a skillfully chosen poetic form, the more inward and imaginative part of Indian character, as Cooper had given permanence to its external and active side. Of Longfellow's dramatic experiments the *Golden Legend*, 1851, alone deserves mention here. This was in his chosen realm; a tale taken from the ecclesiastical annals of the middle ages, precious with martyrs' blood and bathed in the rich twilight of the cloister. It contains some of his best work, but its merit is rather poetic than dramatic; although Ruskin praised it for the closeness with which it entered into the temper of the monk.

Longfellow has pleased the people more than the critics. He gave freely what he had, and the gift was beautiful. Those who have looked in his poetry for something else than poetry, or for poetry of some other kind, have not been slow to assert that he was a lady's poet; one who satisfied callow youths and school-girls by uttering commonplaces in graceful and musical shape, but who offered no strong meat for men. Miss Fuller called his poetry thin and the poet himself a "dandy Pindar." This is not true of his poetry, or of the best of it. But he had a singing and not a talking voice, and in his prose one becomes sensible of a certain weakness. *Hyperion*, for example, published in 1839, a loitering fiction, interspersed with descriptions of European travel, is, upon the whole, a weak book, over flowery in diction and sentimental in tone.

The crown of Longfellow's achievements as a translator was his great version of Dante's *Divina Commedia*, published between 1867 and 1870. It is a severely literal, almost a line for line, rendering. The meter is preserved, but the rhyme sacrificed. If not the best English poem constructed from Dante, it is at all events the most faithful and scholarly paraphrase. The sonnets which accompanied it are among Longfellow's best work. He seems to have been raised by daily communion with the great Tuscan into a habit of deeper and more subtle thought than is elsewhere common in his poetry.

Oliver Wendell Holmes (1809–) is a native of Cambridge and a graduate of Harvard in the class of '29; a class whose anniversary reunions he has celebrated in something like forty distinct poems and songs. For sheer cleverness and versatility Dr. Holmes is, perhaps, unrivaled among American men of letters. He has been poet, wit, humorist, novelist, essayist and a college lecturer and writer on medical topics. In all of these departments he has produced work which ranks high, if not with the highest His father, Dr

Abiel Holmes, was a graduate of Yale and an orthodox minister of liberal temper, but the son early threw in his lot with the Unitarians; and, as was natural to a man of a satiric turn and with a very human enjoyment of a fight, whose youth was cast in an age of theological controversy, he has always had his fling at Calvinism and has prolonged the slogans of old battles into a later generation; sometimes, perhaps, insisting upon them rather wearisomely and beyond the limits of good taste. He had, even as an undergraduate, a reputation for cleverness at writing comic verses, and many of his good things in this kind, such as the *Dorchester Giant* and the *Height of the Ridiculous*, were contributed to the *Collegian*, a students' paper. But he first drew the attention of a wider public by his spirited ballad of *Old Ironsides*—

"Ay! Tear her tattered ensign down!"—

composed about 1830, when it was proposed by the government to take to pieces the unseaworthy hulk of the famous old man-of-war, "Constitution." Holmes's indignant protest—which has been a favorite subject for school-boy declamation—had the effect of postponing the vessel's fate for a great many years. From 1830–35 the young poet was pursuing his medical studies in Boston and Paris, contributing now and then some verses to the magazines. Of his life as a medical student in Paris there are many pleasant reminiscences in his *Autocrat* and other writings, as where he tells, for instance, of a dinner party of Americans in the French capital, where one of the company brought tears of home-sickness into the eyes of his *sodales* by saying that the tinkle of the ice in the champagne-glasses reminded him of the cowbells in the rocky old pastures of New England. In 1836 he printed his first collection of poems. The volume contained among a number of pieces broadly comic, like the *September Gale*, the *Music Grinders*, and the *Ballad of the Oysterman*—which at once became widely popular—a few poems of a finer and quieter temper, in which there was a quaint blending of the humorous and the pathetic. Such were *My Aunt* and the *Last Leaf*—which Abraham Lincoln found "inexpressibly touching," and which it is difficult to read without the double tribute of a smile and a tear. The volume contained also *Poetry: A Metrical Essay*, read before the Harvard Chapter of the Phi Beta Kappa Society, which was the first of that long line of capital occasional poems which Holmes has been spinning for half a century with no sign of fatigue and with scarcely any falling off in freshness; poems read or spoken or sung at all manner of gatherings, public and private; at Harvard commencements, class days, and other academic anniversaries; at inaugurations, centennials, dedications of cemeteries, meetings of medical associations, mercantile libraries, Burns clubs and New England societies; at rural festivals and city fairs; openings of theaters, layings of corner stones, birthday celebrations, jubilees, funerals, commemoration services, dinners of welcome or farewell to Dickens, Bryant, Everett, Whittier, Longfellow, Grant, Farragut, the Grand Duke Alexis, the Chinese Embassy and what not. Probably no poet of any age or clime has written so much and so well to order. He has been particularly happy in verses of a convivial kind, toasts for big civic feasts, or post-prandial rhymes for the *petit comité* —the snug little dinners of the chosen few. His

"The quaint trick to cram the pithy line
That cracks so crisply over bubbling wine."

And although he could write on occasion a *Song for a Temperance Dinner*, he has preferred to chant the praise of the punch bowl and to

"feel the old convivial glow (unaided) o'er me stealing,
The warm, champagny, old-particular-brandy-punchy feeling."

It would be impossible to enumerate the many good things of this sort which Holmes has written, full of wit and wisdom, and of humor lightly dashed with sentiment and sparkling with droll analogies, sudden puns, and unexpected turns of rhyme and phrase. Among the best of them are *Nux Postcoenatica, A Modest Request, Ode for a Social Meeting, The Boys*, and *Rip Van Winkle, M.D.* Holmes's favorite measure, in his longer poems, is the heroic couplet which Pope's example seems to have consecrated forever to satiric and didactic verse. He writes as easily in this meter as if it were prose, and with much of Pope's epigrammatic neatness. He also manages with facility the anapæstics of Moore and the ballad stanza which Hood had made the vehicle for his drolleries. It cannot be expected that verses manufactured to pop with the corks and fizz with the champagne at academic banquets should much outlive the occasion; or that the habit of producing such verses on demand should foster in the producer that "high seriousness" which Matthew Arnold asserts to be one mark of all great poetry. Holmes's poetry is mostly on the colloquial level, excellent society-verse, but even in its serious moments too smart and too pretty to be taken very gravely; with a certain glitter, knowingness and flippancy about it and an absence of that self-forgetfulness and intense absorption in its theme which characterize the work of the higher imagination. This is rather the product of fancy and wit. Wit, indeed, in the old sense of quickness in the perception of analogies is the staple of his mind. His resources in the way of figure, illustration, allusion and anecdote are wonderful. Age cannot wither him nor custom stale his infinite variety, and there is as much powder in his latest pyrotechnics as in the rockets which he sent up half a century ago. Yet, though the humorist in him rather outweighs the poet, he has written a few things, like the *Chambered Nautilus* and *Homesick in Heaven*, which are as purely and deeply poetic as the *One-Hoss Shay* and the *Prologue* are funny.

Dr. Holmes is not of the stuff of which idealists and enthusiasts are made. As a physician and a student of science, the facts of the material universe have counted for much with him. His clear, positive, alert intellect was always impatient of mysticism. He had the sharp eye of the satirist and the man of the world for oddities of dress, dialect and manners. Naturally the transcendental movement struck him on its ludicrous side, and in his *After-Dinner Poem,* read at the Phi Beta Kappa dinner at Cambridge in 1843, he had his laugh at the " Orphic odes " and " runes " of the bedlamite seer and bard of mystery

> " Who rides a beetle which he calls a ' sphinx.'
> And O what questions asked in club-foot rhyme
> Of Earth the tongueless, and the deaf-mute Time !
> Here babbling ' Insight' shouts in Nature's ears
> His last conundrum on the orbs and spheres ;
> There Self-inspection sucks its little thumb,
> With ' Whence am I ? ' and ' Wherefore did I come ? ' "

Curiously enough, the author of these lines lived to write an appreciative life of the poet who wrote the *Sphinx.* There was a good deal of toryism or social conservatism in Holmes. He acknowledged a preference for the man with a pedigree, the man who owned family portraits, had been brought up in familiarity with books, and could pronounce " view " correctly. Readers unhappily not of the " Brahmin caste of New England " have sometimes resented as snobbishness Holmes's harping on "family," and his perpetual application of certain favorite shibboleths to other people's ways of speech. "The woman who calc'lates is lost."

> " Learning condemns beyond the reach of hope
> The careless lips that speak of sŏap for sŏap. . . .
> Do put your accents in the proper spot ;
> Don't, let me beg you, don't say ' How ? ' for ' What ? '
> The things named ' pants ' in certain documents,
> A word not made for gentlemen, but 'gents.' "

With the rest of "society" he was disposed to ridicule the abolition movement as a crotchet of the eccentric and the long-haired. But when the civil war broke out he lent his pen, his tongue, and his own flesh and blood to the cause of the Union. The individuality of Holmes's writings comes in part from their local and provincial bias. He has been the laureate of Harvard College and the bard of Boston city, an urban poet, with a cockneyish fondness for old Boston ways and things—the Common and the Frog Pond, Faneuil Hall and King's Chapel and the Old South, Bunker Hill, Long Wharf, the Tea Party, and the town crier. It was Holmes who invented the playful saying that "Boston State House is the hub of the solar system."

In 1857 was started the *Atlantic Monthly*, a magazine which has published a good share of the best work done by American writers within the past thirty years. Its immediate success was assured by Dr. Holmes's brilliant series of papers, the

Autocrat of the Breakfast Table, 1858, followed at once by the *Professor at the Breakfast Table*, 1859, and later by the *Poet at the Breakfast Table*, 1873. The *Autocrat* is its author's masterpiece, and holds the fine quintessence of his humor, his scholarship, his satire, genial observation, and ripe experience of men and cities. The form is as unique and original as the contents, being something between an essay and a drama; a succession of monologues or table-talks at a typical American boarding-house, with a thread of story running through the whole. The variety of mood and thought is so great that these conversations never tire, and the prose is interspersed with some of the author's choicest verse. The *Professor at the Breakfast Table* followed too closely on the heels of the *Autocrat*, and had less freshness. The third number of the series was better, and was pleasantly reminiscent and slightly garrulous, Dr. Holmes being now (1873) sixty-four years old, and entitled to the gossiping privilege of age. The *personnel* of the Breakfast Table series, such as the landlady and the landlady's daughter and her son, Benjamin Franklin ; the schoolmistress, the young man named John, the Divinity Student, the Kohinoor, the Sculpin, the Scarabæus and the Old Gentleman who sits opposite, are not fully drawn characters, but outlined figures, lightly sketched—as is the Autocrat's wont—by means of some trick of speech, or dress, or feature, but they are quite life-like enough for their purpose, which is mainly to furnish listeners and foils to the eloquence and wit of the chief talker.

In 1860 and 1867 Holmes entered the field of fiction with two "medicated novels," *Elsie Venner* and the *Guardian Angel*. The first of these was a singular tale, whose heroine united with her very fascinating human attributes something of the nature of a serpent; her mother having been bitten by a rattlesnake a few months before the birth of the girl, and kept alive meanwhile by the use of powerful antidotes. The heroine of the *Guardian Angel* inherited lawless instincts from a vein of Indian blood in her ancestry. These two books were studies of certain medico-psychological problems. They preached Dr. Holmes's favorite doctrines of heredity and of the modified nature of moral responsibility by reason of transmitted tendencies which limit the freedom of the will. In *Elsie Venner*, in particular, the weirdly imaginative and speculative character of the leading motive suggests Hawthorne's method in fiction, but the background and the subsidiary figures have a realism that is in abrupt contrast with this, and gives a kind of doubleness and want of keeping to the whole. The Yankee characters, in particular, and the satirical pictures of New England country life are open to the charge of caricature. In the *Guardian Angel* the figure of Byles Gridley, the old scholar, is drawn with thorough sympathy, and though some of his acts are improbable he is, on the whole, Holmes's most vital conception in the region of dramatic creation.

James Russell Lowell (1819–), the foremost of American critics and of living American poets is, like Holmes, a native of Cambridge, and, like Emerson and Holmes, a clergyman's son. In 1855 he succeeded Longfellow as Professor of Modern Languages in Harvard College. Of late years he has held important diplomatic posts, like Everett, Irving, Bancroft, Motley, and other Americans distinguished in letters, having been United States Minister to Spain, and, under two administrations, to the Court of St. James. Lowell is not so spontaneously and exclusively a poet as Longfellow. His fame has been of slower growth, and his popularity with the average reader has never been so great. His appeal has been to the few rather than the many, to an audience of scholars and of the judicious rather than to the "groundlings" of the general public. Nevertheless his verse, though without the evenness, instinctive grace, and unerring good taste of Longfellow's, has more energy and a stronger intellectual fiber; while in prose he is very greatly the superior. His first volume, *A Year's Life*, 1841, gave little promise. In 1843 he started a magazine, the *Pioneer*, which only reached its third number, though it counted among its contributors Hawthorne, Poe, Whittier, and Miss Barrett (afterward Mrs. Browning). A second volume of poems, printed in 1844, showed a distinct advance, in such pieces as the *Shepherd of King Admetus, Rhœcus*, a classical myth, told in excellent blank verse, and the same in subject with one of Landor's polished intaglios; and the *Legend of Britanny*, a narrative poem, which had fine passages, but no firmness in the management of the story. As yet, it was evident, the young poet had not found his theme. This came with the outbreak of the Mexican War, which was unpopular in New England, and which the Free Soil party regarded as a slaveholders' war waged without provocation against a sister republic, and simply for the purpose of extending the area of slavery.

In 1846, accordingly, the *Biglow Papers* began to appear in the *Boston Courier*, and were collected and published in book form in 1848. These were a series of rhymed satires upon the government and the war party, written in the Yankee dialect, and supposed to be the work of Hosea Biglow, a homespun genius in a down-east country town, whose letters to the editor were indorsed and accompanied by the comments of the Rev. Homer Wilbur, A.M., pastor of the First Church in Jaalam, and (prospective) member of many learned societies. The first paper was a derisive address to a recruiting sergeant, with a denunciation of the "nigger-drivin' States" and the "northern dough-faces," a plain hint that the North would do better to secede than to continue doing dirty work for the South, and an expression of those universal peace doctrines which were then in the air, and to which

Longfellow gave se.ious utterance in his *Occulta-tion of Orion.*

> " Ez for war, I call it murder—
> There you hev it plain an' flat:
> I don't want to go no furder
> Than my Testyment for that;
> God hez said so plump an' fairly,
> It's ez long as it is broad,
> An' you've gut to git up airly
> Ef you want to take in God."

The second number was a versified paraphrase of a letter received from Mr. Birdofredom Sawin, "a yung feller of our town that wuz cussed fool enuff to goe atrottin inter Miss Chiff arter a drum and fife," and who finds when he gets to Mexico that

" This kind o' sogerin' aint a mite like our October trainin.' "

Of the subsequent papers the best was, perhaps, *What Mr. Robinson Thinks,* an election ballad, which caused universal laughter, and was on every body's tongue.

The *Biglow Papers* remain Lowell's most original contribution to American literature. They are, all in all, the best political satires in the language, and unequaled as portraitures of the Yankee character, with its 'cuteness, its homely wit, and its latent poetry. Under the racy humor of the dialect—which became in Lowell's hands a medium of literary expression almost as effective as

Burns's Ayrshire Scotch—burned that moral enthusiasm and that hatred of wrong and deification of duty—"Stern daughter of the voice of God"—which, in the tough New England stock, stands instead of the passion in the blood of southern races. Lowell's serious poems on political questions, such as the *Present Crisis, Ode to Freedom,* and the *Capture of Fugitive Slaves,* have the old Puritan fervor, and such lines as

> " They are slaves who dare not be
> In the right with two or three,"

and the passage beginning

> " Truth forever on the scaffold, Wrong forever on the throne,"

became watchwords in the conflict against slavery and disunion. Some of these were published in his volume of 1848 and the collected edition of his poems, in two volumes, issued in 1850. These also included his most ambitious narrative poem, the *Vision of Sir Launfal,* an allegorical and spiritual treatment of one of the legends of the Holy Grail. Lowell's genius was not epical, but lyric and didactic. The merit of *Sir Launfal* is not in the telling of the story, but in the beautiful descriptive episodes, one of which, commencing,

> "And what is so rare as a day in June ?
> Then if ever come perfect days ; "

is as current as any thing that he has written. It is significant of the lack of a natural impulse toward narrative invention in Lowell, that, unlike Longfellow and Holmes, he never tried his hand at a novel. One of the most important parts of a novelist's equipment he certainly possesses; namely, an insight into character, and an ability to delineate it. This gift is seen especially in his sketch of Parson Wilbur, who edited the *Biglow Papers* with a delightfully pedantic introduction, glossary, and notes; in the prose essay *On a Certain Condescension in Foreigners*, and in the uncompleted poem, *Fitz-Adam's Story*. See also the sketch of Captain Underhill in the essay on *New England Two Centuries Ago*.

The *Biglow Papers* when brought out in a volume were prefaced by imaginary notices of the press, including a capital parody of Carlyle, and a reprint from the "Jaalam Independent Blunderbuss," of the first sketch—afterward amplified and enriched—of that perfect Yankee idyl, the *Courtin'*. Between 1862 and 1865 a second series of *Biglow Papers* appeared, called out by the events of the civil war. Some of these, as, for instance, *Jonathan to John*, a remonstrance with England for her unfriendly attitude toward the North, were not inferior to any thing in the earlier series; and others were even superior as poems, equal indeed, in pathos and intensity to any thing that Lowell has written in his professedly serious verse. In such passages the dialect wears rather thin, and there is a certain incongruity between the rustic spelling and the vivid beauty and power and the figurative cast of the phrase in stanzas like the following:

> " Wut's words to them whose faith an' truth
> On war's red techstone rang true metal,
> Who ventered life an' love an' youth
> For the gret prize o' death in battle?
> To him who, deadly hurt, agen
> Flashed on afore the charge's thunder,
> Tippin' with fire the bolt of men
> That rived the rebel line asunder?"

Charles Sumner, a somewhat heavy person, with little sense of humor, wished that the author of the *Biglow Papers* "could have used good English." In the lines just quoted, indeed, the bad English adds nothing to the effect. In 1848 Lowell wrote *A Fable for Critics*, something after the style of Sir John Suckling's *Session of the Poets ;* a piece of rollicking doggerel in which he surveyed the American Parnassus, scattering about headlong fun, sharp satire and sound criticism in equal proportion. Never an industrious workman, like Longfellow, at the poetic craft, but preferring to wait for the mood to seize him, he allowed eighteen years to go by, from 1850 to 1868, before publishing another volume of verse. In the latter year appeared *Under the Willows*, which contains some of his ripest and most perfect work; notably *A Winter Evening Hymn to my Fire*, with its noble and touching close—suggested by, perhaps, at any rate recalling, the dedication of Goethe's *Faust*,

> " Ihr naht euch wieder, schwankende Gestalten ; "

the subtle *Footpath* and *In the Twilight*, the lovely little poems *Auf Wiedersehen* and *After the Funeral*, and a number of spirited political pieces, such as *Villa Franca*, and the *Washers of the Shroud*. This volume contained also his *Ode Recited at the Harvard Commemoration* in 1865. This, although uneven, is one of the finest occasional poems in the language, and the most important contribution which our civil war has made to song. It was charged with the grave emotion of one who not only shared the patriotic grief and exultation of his *alma mater* in the sacrifice of her sons, but who felt a more personal sorrow in the loss of kindred of his own, fallen in the front of battle. Particularly noteworthy in this memorial ode are the tribute to Abraham Lincoln, the third strophe, beginning, "Many loved Truth :" the exordium—"O Beautiful! my Country! ours once more!" and the close of the eighth strophe, where the poet chants of the youthful heroes who

"Come transfigured back,
Secure from change in their high-hearted ways,
Beautiful evermore and with the rays
Of morn on their white Shields of Expectation."

From 1857 to 1862 Lowell edited the *Atlantic Monthly*, and from 1863 to 1872 the *North American Review*. His prose, beginning with an early volume of *Conversations on Some of the Old Poets*, 1844, has consisted mainly of critical essays on individual writers, such as Dante, Chaucer, Spenser.

Emerson, Shakespere, Thoreau, Pope, Carlyle, etc., together with papers of a more miscellaneous kind, like *Witchcraft, New England Two Centuries Ago, My Garden Acquaintance, A Good Word for Winter, Abraham Lincoln*, etc., etc. Two volumes of these were published in 1870 and 1876, under the title *Among My Books*, and another, *My Study Windows*, in 1871. As a literary critic Lowell ranks easily among the first of living writers. His scholarship is thorough, his judgment sure, and he pours out upon his page an unwithholding wealth of knowledge, humor, wit and imagination from the fullness of an overflowing mind. His prose has not the chastened correctness and "low tone" of Matthew Arnold's. It is rich, exuberant, and sometimes over fanciful, running away into excesses of allusion or following the lead of a chance pun so as sometimes to lay itself open to the charge of pedantry and bad taste. Lowell's resources in the way of illustration and comparison are endless, and the readiness of his wit and his delight in using it put many temptations in his way. Purists in style accordingly take offense at his saying that "Milton is the only man who ever got much poetry out of a cataract, and that was a cataract in his eye;" or of his speaking of "a gentleman for whom the bottle before him reversed the wonder of the stereoscope and substituted the Gaston v for the b in binocular," which is certainly a puzzling and roundabout fashion of telling us that he had drunk so much that he saw double. The critics also find fault with his coining such words as "undisprivacied" and with his writing such lines as the famous one —from the *Cathedral*, 1870—

"Spume-sliding down the baffled decuman."

It must be acknowledged that his style lacks the crowning grace of simplicity, but it is precisely by reason of its allusive quality that scholarly readers take pleasure in it. They like a diction that has stuff in it and is woven thick, and where a thing is said in such a way as to recall many other things.

Mention should be made, in connection with this Cambridge circle, of one writer who touched its circumference briefly. This was Sylvester Judd, a graduate of Yale, who entered the Harvard Divinity School in 1837 and in 1840 became minister of a Unitarian church in Augusta, Maine. Judd published several books, but the only one of them at all rememberable was *Margaret*, 1845, a novel of which Lowell said in *A Fable for Critics* that it was "the first Yankee book with the soul of Down East in it." It was very imperfect in point of art, and its second part—a rhapsodical description of a sort of Unitarian Utopia—is quite unreadable. But in the delineation of the few chief characters and of the rude, wild life of an outlying New England township just after the close of the revolutionary war, as well as in the tragic power of the catastrophe, there was genius of a high order.

As the country has grown older and more populous, and works in all departments of thought have multiplied, it becomes necessary to draw more strictly the line between the literature of knowledge and the literature of power. Political history, in and of itself, scarcely falls within the limits of this sketch, and yet it cannot be altogether dismissed; for the historian's art at its highest demands imagination, narrative skill, and a sense of unity and proportion in the selection and arrangement of his facts, all of which are literary qualities. It is significant that many of our best historians have begun authorship in the domain of imaginative literature : Bancroft with an early volume of poems; Motley with his historical romances *Merry Mount* and *Morton's Hope*; and Parkman with a novel, *Vassall Morton.* The oldest of that modern group of writers that have given America an honorable position in the historical literature of the world was William Hickling Prescott (1796-1859.) Prescott chose for his theme the history of the Spanish conquests in the New World, a subject full of romantic incident and susceptible of that glowing and perhaps slightly over gorgeous coloring which he laid on with a liberal hand. His completed histories, in their order, are the *Reign of Ferdinand and Isabella*, 1837; the *Conquest of Mexico*, 1843—a topic which Irving had relinquished to him ; and the *Conquest of Peru*, 1847. Prescott was fortunate in being born to leisure and fortune, but he had difficulties of another kind to overcome. He was nearly blind, and had to teach himself Spanish and look up authorities through the help of others and to write with a noctograph or by amanuenses.

George Bancroft (1800-   ) issued the first volume of his great *History of the United States* in 1834, and exactly half a century later the final volume of the work, bringing the subject down to 1789. Bancroft had studied at Göttingen and imbibed from the German historian Heeren the scientific method of historical study. He had access to original sources, in the nature of collections and state papers in the governmental archives of Europe, of which no American had hitherto been able to avail himself. His history in thoroughness of treatment leaves nothing to be desired, and has become the standard authority on the subject. As a literary performance merely, it is somewhat wanting in flavor, Bancroft's manner being heavy and stiff when compared with Motley's or Parkman's. The historian's services to his country have been publicly recognized by his successive appointments as Secretary of the Navy, Minister to England, and Minister to Germany.

The greatest, on the whole, of American historians was John Lothrop Motley (1814–1877), who, like Bancroft, was a student at Göttingen and United States Minister to England. His *Rise of the Dutch Republic*, 1856, and *History of the United Netherlands*, published in installments from 1861 to

1868, equaled Bancroft's work in scientific thoroughness and philosophic grasp, and Prescott's in the picturesque brilliancy of the narrative, while it excelled them both in its masterly analysis of great historic characters, reminding the reader, in this particular, of Macaulay's figure painting. The episodes of the siege of Antwerp and the sack of the cathedral, and of the defeat and wreck of the Spanish Armada, are as graphic as Prescott's famous description of Cortez's capture of the city of Mexico; while the elder historian has nothing to compare with Motley's vivid personal sketches of Queen Elizabeth, Philip the Second, Henry of Navarre, and William the Silent. The *Life of John of Barneveld*, 1874, completed this series of studies upon the history of the Netherlands, a theme to which Motley was attracted because the heroic struggle of the Dutch for liberty offered, in some respects, a parallel to the growth of political independence in Anglo-Saxon communities, and especially in his own America.

The last of these Massachusetts historical writers whom we shall mention is Francis Parkman (1823–), whose subject has the advantage of being thoroughly American. His *Oregon Trail*, 1847, a series of sketches of prairie and Rocky Mountain life, originally contributed to the *Knickerbocker Magazine*, displays his early interest in the American Indians. In 1851 appeared his first historical work, the *Conspiracy of Pontiac*. This has been followed by the series entitled *France and England in North America*, the six successive parts of which are as follows: the *Pioneers of France in the New World;* the *Jesuits in North America; La Salle and the Discovery of the Great West;* the *Old Régime in Canada; Count Frontenac and New France;* and *Montcalm and Wolfe.* These narratives have a wonderful vividness, and a romantic interest not inferior to Cooper's novels. Parkman made himself personally familiar with the scenes which he described, and some of the best descriptions of American woods and waters are to be found in his histories. If any fault is to be found with his books, indeed, it is that their picturesqueness and "fine writing" are a little in excess.

The political literature of the years from 1837 to 1861 hinged upon the antislavery struggle. In this "irrepressible conflict" Massachusetts led the van. Garrison had written in his *Liberator*, in 1830, "I will be as harsh as truth and as uncompromising as justice. I am in earnest; I will not equivocate; I will not excuse; I will not retreat a single inch; and I will be heard." But the Garrisonian abolitionists remained for a long time, even in the North, a small and despised faction. It was a great point gained when men of education and social standing like Wendell Phillips (1811-1884), and Charles Sumner (1811-1874), joined themselves to the cause. Both of these were graduates of Harvard and men of scholarly pursuits. They became the representative orators of the antislavery party, Phillips on the platform and Sumner in the Senate. The former first came before the public in his fiery speech, delivered in Faneuil Hall December 8, 1837, before a meeting called to denounce the murder of Lovejoy, who had been killed at Alton, Ill., while defending his press against a pro-slavery mob. Thenceforth Phillips's voice was never idle in behalf of the slave. His eloquence was impassioned and direct, and his English singularly pure, simple, and nervous. He is perhaps nearer to Demosthenes than any other American orator. He was a most fascinating platform speaker on themes outside of politics, and his lecture on the *Lost Arts* was a favorite with audiences of all sorts.

Sumner was a man of intellectual tastes, who entered politics reluctantly, and only in obedience to the resistless leading of his conscience. He was a student of literature and art; a connoisseur of engravings, for example, of which he made a valuable collection. He was fond of books, conversation, and foreign travel, and in Europe, while still a young man, had made a remarkable impression in society. But he left all this for public life, and in 1851 was elected, as Webster's successor, to the Senate of the United States. Thereafter he remained the leader of the Abolitionists in Congress until slavery was abolished. His influence throughout the North was greatly increased by the brutal attack upon him in the Senate chamber in 1856 by "Bully Brooks" of South Carolina. Sumner's oratory was stately and somewhat labored. While speaking he always seemed, as has been wittily said, to be surveying a "broad landscape of his own convictions." His most impressive qualities as a speaker were his intense moral earnestness and his thorough knowledge of his subject. The most telling of his parliamentary speeches are perhaps his speech *On the Kansas-Nebraska Bill*, of February 3, 1854, and *On the Crime against Kansas*, May 19 and 20, 1856; of his platform addresses, the oration on the *True Grandeur of Nations*.

1. Henry Wadsworth Longfellow. Voices of the Night. The Skeleton in Armor. The Wreck of the Hesperus. The Village Blacksmith. The Belfry of Bruges and Other Poems (1846). By the Seaside. Hiawatha. Tales of a Wayside Inn.

2. Oliver Wendell Holmes. Autocrat of the Breakfast Table. Elsie Venner. Old Ironsides. The Last Leaf. My Aunt. The Music-Grinders. On Lending a Punch Bowl. Nux Postcoenatica. A Modest Request. The Living Temple. Meeting of the Alumni of Harvard College. Homesick in Heaven. Epilogue to the Breakfast Table Series. The Boys. Dorothy. The Iron Gate.

3. James Russell Lowell. The Biglow Papers (two series). Under the Willows and Other Poems. 1868. Rhœcus. The Shepherd of King Admetus. The Vision of Sir Launfal. The Pres-

ent Crisis. The Dandelion. The Birch Tree. Beaver Brook. Essays on Chaucer: Shakspere Once More: Dryden: Emerson: the Lecturer: Thoreau: My Garden Acquaintance: A Good Word for Winter: A Certain Condescension in Foreigners.

4. William Hickling Prescott. The Conquest of Mexico.

5. John Lothrop Motley. The United Netherlands.

6. Francis Parkman. The Oregon Trail. The Jesuits in North America.

7. Representative American Orations; volume v. Edited by Alexander Johnston. New York: G. P. Putnam's Sons. 1884.

CHAPTER VI.
LITERATURE IN THE CITIES.
1837-1861.

LITERATURE as a profession has hardly existed in the United States until very recently. Even now the number of those who support themselves by purely literary work is small, although the growth of the reading public and the establishment of great magazines, such as *Harper's*, the *Century*, and the *Atlantic*, have made a market for intellectual wares which forty years ago would have seemed a godsend to poorly paid Bohemians like Poe or obscure men of genius like Hawthorne. About 1840 two Philadelphia magazines—*Godey's Lady's Book* and *Graham's Monthly*—began to pay their contributors twelve dollars a page, a price then thought wildly munificent. But the first magazine of the modern type was *Harper's Monthly*, founded in 1850. American books have always suffered, and still continue to suffer, from the want of an international copyright, which has flooded the country with cheap reprints and translations of foreign works, with which the domestic product has been unable to contend on such uneven terms. With the first ocean steamers there started up a class of large-paged weeklies in New York and elsewhere, such as *Brother Jonathan*, the *New World*, and the *Corsair*, which furnished their readers with the freshest writings of Dickens and Bulwer and other British celebrities within a fortnight after their appearance in London. This still further restricted the profits of native authors and nearly drove them from the field of periodical literature. By special arrangement the novels of Thackeray and other English writers were printed in *Harper's* in installments simultaneously with their issue in English periodicals. The *Atlantic* was the first of our magazines which was founded expressly for the encouragement, of home talent, and which had a purely Yankee flavor. Journalism was the profession which naturally attracted men of letters, as having most in common with their chosen work and as giving them a medium, under their own control, through which they could address the public. A few favored scholars, like Prescott, were made independent by the possession of private fortunes. Others, like Holmes, Longfellow, and Lowell, gave to literature such leisure as they could get in the intervals of an active profession or of college work. Still others, like Emerson and Thoreau, by living in the country and making their modest competence — eked out in Emerson's case by lecturing here and there—suffice for their simple needs, secured themselves freedom from the restraints of any regular calling. But in default of some such *pou sto* our men of letters have usually sought the cities and allied themselves with the press. It will be remembered that Lowell started a short-lived magazine on his own account, and that he afterward edited the *Atlantic* and the *North American*. Also that Ripley and Charles A. Dana betook themselves to journalism after the break up of the Brook Farm Community.

In the same way William Cullen Bryant (1794–1878), the earliest American poet of importance, whose impulses drew him to the solitudes of nature, was compelled to gain a livelihood by conducting a daily newspaper; or, as he himself puts it, was

> "Forced to drudge for the dregs of men,
> And scrawl strange words with the barbarous pen."

Bryant was born at Cummington, in Berkshire, the westernmost county of Massachusetts. After two years in Williams College he studied law, and practiced for nine years as a country lawyer in Plainfield and Great Barrington. Following the line of the Housatonic Valley, the social and theological affiliations of Berkshire have always been closer with Connecticut and New York than with Boston and Eastern Massachusetts. Accordingly, when, in 1825, Bryant yielded to the attractions of a literary career, he betook himself to New York city, where, after a brief experiment in conducting a monthly magazine, the *New York Review and Athenæum*, he assumed the editorship of the *Even-*

ing Post, a Democratic and Free-trade journal, with which he remained connected till his death. He already had a reputation as a poet when he entered the ranks of metropolitan journalism. In 1816 his *Thanatopsis* had been published in the *North American Review,* and had attracted immediate and general admiration. It had been finished, indeed, two years before, when the poet was only in his nineteenth year, and was a wonderful instance of precocity. The thought in this stately hymn was not that of a young man, but of a sage who has reflected long upon the universality, the necessity, and the majesty of death. Bryant's blank verse when at its best, as in *Thanatopsis* and the *Forest Hymn,* is extremely noble. In gravity and dignity it is surpassed by no English blank verse of this century, though in rich and various modulation it falls below Tennyson's *Ulysses* and *Morte d'Arthur.* It was characteristic of Bryant's limitations that he came thus early into possession of his faculty. His range was always a narrow one; and about his poetry, as a whole, there is a certain coldness, rigidity, and solemnity. His fixed position among American poets is described in his own *Hymn to the North Star*:

" And thou dost see them rise,
  Star of the pole ! and thou dost see them set.
Alone, in thy cold skies,
  Thou keep'st thy old, unmoving station yet,
  Nor join'st the dances of that glittering train,
  Nor dipp'st thy virgin orb in the blue western main."

In 1821 he read the *Ages*, a didactic poem in thirty-five stanzas, before the Phi Beta Kappa Society at Cambridge, and in the same year brought out his first volume of poems. A second collection appeared in 1832, which was printed in London under the auspices of Washington Irving. Bryant was the first American poet who had much of an audience in England, and Wordsworth is said to have learned *Thanatopsis* by heart. Bryant was, indeed, in a measure, a scholar of Wordsworth's school, and his place among American poets corresponds roughly, though not precisely, to Wordsworth's among English poets. With no humor, with somewhat restricted sympathies, with little flexibility or openness to new impressions, but gifted with a high, austere imagination, Bryant became the meditative poet of nature. His best poems are those in which he draws lessons from nature, or sings of its calming, purifying, and bracing influences upon the human soul. His office, in other words, is the same which Matthew Arnold asserts to be the peculiar office of modern poetry, "the moral interpretation of nature." Poems of this class are *Green River*, *To a Waterfowl*, *June*, the *Death of the Flowers*, and the *Evening Wind*. The song, "O fairest of the Rural Maids," which has more fancy than is common in Bryant, and which Poe pronounced his best poem, has an obvious resemblance to Wordsworth's "Three years she grew in sun and shade," and both of these nameless pieces might fitly be entitled—as Wordsworth's is in Mr. Palgrave's *Golden Treasury*—" The Education of Nature."

Although Bryant's career is identified with New York, his poetry is all of New England. His heart was always turning back fondly to the woods and streams of the Berkshire hills. There was nothing of that urban strain in him which appears in Holmes and Willis. He was, in especial, the poet of autumn, of the American October and the New England Indian Summer, that season of "dropping nuts" and "smoky light," to whose subtle analogy with the decay of the young by the New England disease, consumption, he gave such tender expression in the *Death of the Flowers;* and amid whose "bright, late quiet," he wished himself to pass away. Bryant is our poet of "the melancholy days," as Lowell is of June. If, by chance, he touches upon June, it is not with the exultant gladness of Lowell in meadows full of bobolinks, and in the summer day that is

> "—simply perfect from its own resource
> As to the bee the new campanula's
> Illuminate seclusion swung in air."

Rather, the stir of new life in the clod suggests to Bryant by contrast the thought of death; and there is nowhere in his poetry a passage of deeper feeling than the closing stanzas of *June*, in which he speaks of himself, by anticipation, as of one

> "Whose part in all the pomp that fills
> The circuit of the summer hills
> Is—that his grave is green."

Bryant is, *par excellence*, the poet of New England wild flowers, the yellow violet, the fringed gentian —to each of which he dedicated an entire poem— the orchis and the golden rod, "the aster in the wood and the yellow sunflower by the brook." With these his name will be associated as Wordsworth's with the daffodil and the lesser celandine, and Emerson's with the rhodora.

Except when writing of nature he was apt to be commonplace, and there are not many such energetic lines in his purely reflective verse as these famous ones from the *Battle Field:*

> " Truth crushed to earth shall rise again;
> The eternal years of God are hers ;
> But Error, wounded, writhes in pain,
> And dies among his worshipers."

He added but slowly to the number of his poems, publishing a new collection in 1840, another in 1844, and *Thirty Poems* in 1864. His work at all ages was remarkably even. *Thanatopsis* was as mature as any thing that he wrote afterward, and among his later pieces, the *Planting of the Apple Tree* and the *Flood of Years* were as fresh as any thing that he had written in the first flush of youth. Bryant's poetic style was always pure and correct, without any tincture of affectation or extravagance. His prose writings are not important, consisting mainly of papers of the *Salmagundi* variety contributed to the *Talisman*, an annual published in 1827–30; some rather sketchy stories, *Tales of the*

Glauber Spa, 1832; and impressions of Europe, entitled, *Letters of a Traveler*, issued in two series, in 1849 and 1858. In 1869 and 1871 appeared his blank-verse translations of the *Iliad* and *Odyssey*, a remarkable achievement for a man of his age, and not excelled, upon the whole, by any recent metrical version of Homer in the English tongue Bryant's half century of service as the editor of a daily paper should not be overlooked. The *Evening Post*, under his management, was always honest, gentlemanly, and courageous, and did much to raise the tone of journalism in New York.

Another Massachusetts poet, who was outside the Boston coterie, like Bryant, and, like him, tried his hand at journalism, was John Greenleaf Whittier (1807-). He was born in a solitary farmhouse near Haverhill, in the valley of the Merrimack, and his life has been passed mostly at his native place and at the neighboring town of Amesbury. The local color, which is very pronounced in his poetry, is that of the Merrimack from the vicinity of Haverhill to its mouth at Newburyport, a region of hillside farms, opening out below into wide marshes— "the low, green prairies of the sea," and the beaches of Hampton and Salisbury. The scenery of the Merrimack is familiar to all readers of Whittier: the cotton-spinning towns along its banks, with their factories and dams, the sloping pastures and orchards of the back country, the sands of Plum Island and the level reaches of water meadow between which glide the broad-sailed "gundalows"—

a local corruption of gondola—laden with hay. Whittier was a farmer lad, and had only such education as the district school could supply, supplemented by two years at the Haverhill Academy. In his *School Days* he gives a picture of the little old country school-house as it used to be, the only *alma mater* of so many distinguished Americans, and to which many others who have afterward trodden the pavements of great universities look back so fondly as to their first wicket gate into the land of knowledge.

> "Still sits the school-house by the road,
>   A ragged beggar sunning;
> Around it still the sumachs grow
>   And blackberry vines are running.
>
> "Within, the master's desk is seen,
>   Deep-scarred by raps official;
> The warping floor, the battered seats,
>   The jack-knife's carved initial."

A copy of Burns awoke the slumbering instinct in the young poet, and he began to contribute verses to Garrison's *Free Press*, published at Newburyport, and to the *Haverhill Gazette*. Then he went to Boston, and became editor for a short time of the *Manufacturer*. Next he edited the *Essex Gazette*, at Haverhill, and in 1830 he took charge of George D. Prentice's paper, the *New England Weekly Review*, at Hartford, Conn. Here he fell in with a young Connecticut poet of much promise, J. G. C. Brainard, editor of the *Connecti-

cut Mirror, whose "Remains" Whittier edited in 1832. At Hartford, too, he published his first book, a volume of prose and verse, entitled *Legends of New England*, 1831, which is not otherwise remarkable than as showing his early interest in Indian colonial traditions—especially those which had a touch of the supernatural—a mine which he afterward worked to good purpose in the *Bridal of Pennacook*, the *Witch's Daughter*, and similar poems. Some of the *Legends* testify to Brainard's influence and to the influence of Whittier's temporary residence at Hartford. One of the prose pieces, for example, deals with the famous "Moodus Noises" at Haddam, on the Connecticut River, and one of the poems is the same in subject with Brainard's *Black Fox of Salmon River*. After a year and a half at Hartford, Whittier returned to Haverhill and to farming.

The antislavery agitation was now beginning, and into this he threw himself with all the ardor of his nature. He became the poet of the reform as Garrison was its apostle, and Sumner and Phillips its speakers. In 1833 he published *Justice and Expediency*, a prose tract against slavery, and in the same year he took part in the formation of the American Antislavery Society at Philadelphia, sitting in the convention as a delegate of the Boston Abolitionists. Whittier was a Quaker, and that denomination, influenced by the preaching of John Woolman and others, had long since quietly abolished slavery within its own communion. The

Quakers of Philadelphia and elsewhere took an earnest though peaceful part in the Garrisonian movement. But it was a strange irony of fate that had made the fiery-hearted Whittier a Friend. His poems against slavery and disunion have the martial ring of a Tyrtæus or a Körner, added to the stern religious zeal of Cromwell's Ironsides. They are like the sound of the trumpet blown before the walls of Jericho, or the Psalms of David denouncing woe upon the enemies of God's chosen people. If there is any purely Puritan strain in American poetry it is in the war-hymns of the Quaker "Hermit of Amesbury." Of these patriotic poems there were three principal collections: *Voices of Freedom*, 1849; the *Panorama and Other Poems*, 1856; and *In War Time*, 1863; Whittier's work as the poet of freedom was done when, on hearing the bells ring for the passage of the constitutional amendment abolishing slavery, he wrote his splendid *Laus Deo*, thrilling with the ancient Hebrew spirit:

> "Loud and long
> Lift the old exulting song,
>   Sing with Miriam by the sea—
> He has cast the mighty down,
> Horse and rider sink and drown,
>   He hath triumphed gloriously."

Of his poems distinctly relating to the events of the civil war, the best, or at all events the most popular, is *Barbara Frietchie*. *Ichabod*, expressing the indignation of the Free Soilers at Daniel Webster's seventh of March speech in defense of the

Fugitive Slave Law, is one of Whittier's best political poems, and not altogether unworthy of comparison with Browning's *Lost Leader*. The language of Whittier's warlike lyrics is biblical, and many of his purely devotional pieces are religious poetry of a high order and have been included in numerous collections of hymns. Of his songs of faith and doubt, the best are perhaps *Our Master*, *Chapel of the Hermits*, and *Eternal Goodness ;* one stanza from the last of which is familiar :

"I know not where His islands lift
 Their fronded palms in air,
I only know I cannot drift
 Beyond His love and care."

But from politics and war Whittier turned gladly to sing the homely life of the New England country side. His rural ballads and idyls are as genuinely American as any thing that our poets have written, and have been recommended, as such, to English working-men by Whittier's co-religionist, John Bright. The most popular of these is probably *Maud Muller*, whose closing couplet has passed into proverb. *Skipper Ireson's Ride* is also very current. Better than either of them, as poetry, is *Telling the Bees*. But Whittier's masterpiece in work of a descriptive and reminiscent kind is *Snow Bound*, 1866, a New England fireside idyl which in its truthfulness recalls the *Winter Evening* of Cowper's *Task* and Burns's *Cotter's Saturday Night*, but in sweetness and animation is superior to either of them. Although in some things a Puritan of the Puritans, Whittier has never forgotten that he is also a Friend, and several of his ballads and songs have been upon the subject of the early Quaker persecutions in Massachusetts. The most impressive of these is *Cassandra Southwick*. The latest of them, the *King's Missive*, originally contributed to the *Memorial History of Boston* in 1880, and reprinted the next year in a volume with other poems, has been the occasion of a rather lively controversy. The *Bridal of Pennacook*, 1848, and the *Tent on the Beach*, 1867, which contain some of his best work, were series of ballads told by different narrators, after the fashion of Longfellow's *Tales of a Wayside Inn*. As an artist in verse Whittier is strong and fervid, rather than delicate or rich. He uses only a few metrical forms—by preference the eight-syllabled rhyming couplet

—"Maud Muller on a summer's day
Raked the meadow sweet with hay," etc.—

and the emphatic tramp of this measure becomes very monotonous, as do some of Whittier's mannerisms; which proceed, however, never from affectation, but from a lack of study and variety, and so, no doubt, in part from the want of that academic culture and thorough technical equipment which Lowell and Longfellow enjoyed. Though his poems are not in dialect, like Lowell's *Biglow Papers*, he knows how to make an artistic use of homely provincial words, such as "chore," which give his idyls of the hearth and the barnyard a genuine Doric cast. Whittier's prose is inferior to his verse. The fluency which was a besetting sin of his poetry when released from the fetters of rhyme and meter ran into wordiness His prose writings were partly contributions to the slavery controversy, partly biographical sketches of English and American reformers, and partly studies of the scenery and folk-lore of the Merrimack Valley. Those of most literary interest were the *Supernaturalism of New England*, 1847, and some of the papers in *Literary Recreations and Miscellanies*, 1854.

While Massachusetts was creating an American literature, other sections of the Union were by no means idle. The West, indeed, was as yet too raw to add any thing of importance to the artistic product of the country. The South was hampered by circumstances which will presently be described. But in and about the seaboard cities of New York, Philadelphia, Baltimore and Richmond, many pens were busy filling the columns of literary weeklies and monthlies; and there was a considerable output, such as it was, of books of poetry, fiction, travel, and miscellaneous light literature. Time has already relegated most of these to the dusty topshelves. To rehearse the names of the numerous contributors to the old *Knickerbocker Magazine*, to *Godey's*, and *Graham's*, and the *New Mirror*, and the *Southern Literary Messenger*, or to run over the list of authorlings and poetasters in Poe's papers on the *Literati of New York*, would be very much like reading the inscriptions on the head-stones of an old grave-yard. In the columns of these prehistoric magazines and in the book notices and reviews away back in the thirties and forties, one encounters the handiwork and the names of Emerson, Holmes, Longfellow, Hawthorne, and Lowell, embodied in this mass of forgotten literature. It would have required a good deal of critical acumen, at the time, to predict that these and a few others would soon be thrown out into bold relief, as the significant and permanent names in the literature of their generation, while Paulding, Hirst, Fay, Dawes, Mrs. Osgood, and scores of others who figured beside them in the fashionable periodicals, and filled quite as large a space in the public eye, would sink into oblivion in less than thirty years. Some of these latter were clever enough people; they entertained their contemporary public sufficiently, but their work had no vitality or "power of continuance." The great majority of the writings of any period are necessarily ephemeral, and time by a slow process of natural selection is constantly sifting out the few representative books which shall carry on the memory of the period to posterity. Now and then it may be predicted of some undoubted work of genius, even at the moment that it sees the light, that it is destined to endure. But tastes and fashions change, and few things are better calculated to inspire the literary critic with humility than to read the prophecies in old reviews and see how the future, now become the present, has quietly given them the lie.

From among the professional *littérateurs* of his day emerges, with ever sharper distinctness as time goes on, the name of Edgar Allan Poe (1809-1849.) By the irony of fate Poe was born at Boston, and his first volume, *Tamerlane and Other Poems*, 1827, was printed in that city and bore upon its title page the words, "By a Bostonian." But his parentage, so far as it was any thing, was southern. His father was a Marylander who had gone upon the stage and married an actress, herself the daughter of an actress and a native of England. Left an orphan by the early death of both parents, Poe was adopted by a Mr. Allan, a wealthy merchant of Richmond, Va. He was educated partly at an English school, was student for a time in the University of Virginia and afterward a cadet in the Military Academy at West Point. His youth was wild and irregular: he gambled and drank, was proud, bitter and perverse; finally quarreled with his guardian and adopted father—by whom he was disowned—and then betook himself to the life of a literary hack. His brilliant but underpaid work for various periodicals soon brought him into notice, and he was given the editorship of the *Southern Literary Messenger*, published at Richmond, and subsequently of the *Gentlemen's*—afterward *Graham's*—*Magazine* in Philadelphia. These and all other positions Poe forfeited through his dissipated habits and wayward temper, and finally, in 1844, he drifted to New York, where he found employment on the *Evening Mirror* and then on the *Broadway Journal.* He died of delirium tremens at the Marine Hospital in Baltimore. His life was one of the most wretched in literary history. He was an extreme instance of what used to be called the "eccentricity of genius." He had the irritable vanity which is popularly supposed to accompany the poetic temperament, and was so insanely egotistic as to imagine that Longfellow and others were constantly plagiarizing from him. The best side of Poe's character came out in his domestic relations, in which he displayed great tenderness, patience and fidelity. His instincts were gentlemanly, and his manner and conversation were often winning. In the place of moral feeling he had the artistic conscience. In his critical papers, except where warped by passion or prejudice, he showed neither fear nor favor, denouncing bad work by the most illustrious hands and commending obscure merit. The "impudent literary cliques" who puffed each other's books; the feeble chirrupings of the bardlings who manufactured verses for the " Annuals ; " and the twaddle of the " genial " incapables who praised them in flabby reviews—all these Poe exposed with ferocious honesty. Nor, though his writings are *un*moral, can they be called in any sense *im*moral. His poetry is as pure in its unearthliness as Bryant's in its austerity.

By 1831 Poe had published three thin books of verse, none of which had attracted notice, although the latest contained the drafts of a few of his most perfect poems, such as *Israfel*, the *Valley of Unrest*, the *City in the Sea*, and one of the two pieces inscribed *To Helen*. It was his habit to touch and retouch his work until it grew under his more practiced hand into a shape that satisfied his fastidious taste. Hence the same poem frequently reappears in different stages of development in successive editions. Poe was a subtle artist in the realm of the weird and the fantastic. In his intellectual nature there was a strange conjunction; an imagination as spiritual as Shelley's, though, unlike Shelley's, haunted perpetually with shapes of fear and the imagery of ruin; with this, an analytic power, a scientific exactness, and a mechanical ingenuity more usual in a chemist or a mathematician than in a poet. He studied carefully the mechanism of his verse and experimented endlessly with verbal and musical effects, such as repetition, and monotone, and the selection of words in which the consonants alliterated and the vowels varied. In his *Philosophy of Composition* he described how his best known poem, the *Raven*, was systematically built up on a preconceived plan in which the number of lines was first determined and the word "nevermore" selected as a starting-point. No one who knows the mood in which poetry is composed will believe that this ingenious piece of dissection really describes the way in which the *Raven* was conceived and written, or that any such deliberate and self-conscious process could *originate* the associations from which a true poem springs. But it flattered Poe's pride of intellect to assert that his cooler reason had control not only over the execution of his poetry, but over the very well-head of thought and emotion. Some of his most successful stories, like the *Gold Bug*, the *Mystery of Marie Roget*, the *Purloined Letter*, and the *Murders in the Rue Morgue*, were applications of this analytic faculty to the solution of puzzles, such as the finding of buried treasure or of a lost document, or the ferreting out of a mysterious crime. After the publication of the *Gold Bug* he received from all parts of the country specimens of cipher writing, which he delighted to work out. Others of his tales were clever pieces of mystification, like *Hans Pfaall*, the story of a journey to the moon, or experiments at giving verisimilitude to wild improbabilities by the skillful introduction of scientific details, as in the *Facts in the Case of M. Valdemar* and *Von Kempelen's Discovery*. In his narratives of this kind Poe anticipated the detective novels of Gaboriau and Wilkie Collins, the scientific hoaxes of Jules Verne, and, though in a less degree, the artfully worked up likeness to fact in Edward Everett Hale's *Man Without a Country*, and similar fictions. While Dickens's *Barnaby Rudge* was publishing in parts, Poe showed his skill as a plot hunter by publishing a paper in *Graham's Magazine* in which the very tangled intrigue of the novel was correctly raveled and the *finale* predicted in advance.

In his union of imagination and analytic power Poe resembled Coleridge, who, if any one, was his teacher in poetry and criticism. Poe's verse often reminds one of *Christabel* and the *Ancient Mariner*, still oftener of *Kubla Khan.* Like Coleridge, too, he indulged at times in the opium habit. But in Poe the artist predominated over every thing else. He began not with sentiment or thought, but with technique, with melody and color, tricks of language, and effects of verse. It is curious to study the growth of his style in his successive volumes of poetry. At first these are metrical experiments and vague images, original, and with a fascinating suggestiveness, but with so little meaning that some of his earlier pieces are hardly removed from nonsense. Gradually, like distant music drawing nearer and nearer, his poetry becomes fuller of imagination and of an inward significance, without ever losing, however, its mysterious aloofness from the real world of the senses. It was a part of Poe's literary creed—formed upon his own practice and his own limitations, but set forth with a great display of *a priori* reasoning in his essay on the *Poetic Principle* and elsewhere— that pleasure and not instruction or moral exhortation was the end of poetry; that beauty and not truth or goodness was its means; and, furthermore, that the pleasure which it gave should be *indefinite*. About his own poetry there was always this indefiniteness. His imagination dwelt in a strange country of dream — a "ghoul-haunted region of Weir," "out of space, out of time"—filled with unsubstantial landscapes, and peopled by spectral shapes. And yet there is a wonderful, hidden significance in this uncanny scenery. The reader feels that the wild, fantasmal imagery is in itself a kind of language, and that it in some way expresses a brooding thought or passion, the terror and despair of a lost soul. Sometimes there is an obvious allegory, as in the *Haunted Palace*, which is the parable of a ruined mind, or in the *Raven*, the most popular of all Poe's poems, originally published in the *American Whig Review* for February, 1845. Sometimes the meaning is more obscure, as in *Ulalume*, which, to most people, is quite incomprehensible, and yet to all readers of poetic feeling is among the most characteristic, and, therefore, the most fascinating, of its author's creations.

Now and then, as in the beautiful ballad, *Annabel Lee*, and *To One in Paradise*, the poet emerges into the light of common human feeling and speaks a more intelligible language. But in general his poetry is not the poetry of the heart, and its passion is not the passion of flesh and blood. In Poe the thought of death is always near, and of the shadowy borderland between death and life.

"The play is the tragedy 'Man,'
And its hero the Conqueror Worm,"

The prose tale, *Ligeia*, in which these verses are inserted, is one of the most powerful of all Poe's writings, and its theme is the power of the will to overcome death. In that singularly impressive poem, the *Sleeper*, the morbid horror which invests the tomb springs from the same source, the materiality of Poe's imagination, which refuses to let the soul go free from the body.

This quality explains why Poe's *Tales of the Grotesque and Arabesque*, 1840, are on a lower plane than Hawthorne's romances, to which a few of them, like *William Wilson* and the *Man of the Crowd*, have some resemblance. The former of these, in particular, is in Hawthorne's peculiar province, the allegory of the conscience. But in general the tragedy in Hawthorne is a spiritual one, while Poe calls in the aid of material forces. The passion of physical fear or of superstitious horror is that which his writings most frequently excite. These tales represent various grades of the frightful and the ghastly, from the mere bug-a-boo story like the *Black Cat*, which makes children afraid to go in the dark, up to the breathless terror of the *Cask of Amontillado*, or the *Red Death*. Poe's masterpiece in this kind is the fateful tale of the *Fall of the House of Usher*, with its solemn and magnificent close. His prose, at its best, often recalls, in its richly imaginative cast, the manner of De Quincey in such passages as his *Dream Fugue*, or *Our Ladies of Sorrow*. In descriptive pieces like the *Domain of Arnheim*, and stories of adventure like the *Descent into the Maelstrom*, and his long sea tale, *The Narrative of Arthur Gordon Pym*, 1838, he displayed a realistic inventiveness almost equal to Swift's or De Foe's. He was not without a mocking irony, but he had no constructive humor, and his attempts at the facetious were mostly failures.

Poe's magical creations were rootless flowers. He took no hold upon the life about him, and cared nothing for the public concerns of his country. His poems and tales might have been written *in vacuo* for any thing American in them. Perhaps for this reason, in part, his fame has been so cosmopolitan. In France especially his writings have been favorites. Charles Baudelaire, the author of the *Fleurs du Mal*, translated them into French, and his own impressive but unhealthy poetry shows evidence of Poe's influence. The defect in Poe was in character, a defect which will make itself felt in art as in life. If he had had the sweet home feeling of Longfellow or the moral fervor of Whittier he might have been a greater poet than either.

> "If I could dwell
> Where Israfel
>   Hath dwelt, and he where I,
> He might not sing so wildly well
>   A mortal melody,
> While a bolder note than this might swell
>   From my lyre within the sky!"

Though Poe was a southerner, if not by birth, at least by race and breeding, there was nothing distinctly southern about his peculiar genius, and in his wandering life he was associated as much with Philadelphia and New York as with Baltimore and Richmond. The conditions which had made the southern colonies unfruitful in literary and educational works before the Revolution continued to act down to the time of the civil war. Eli Whitney's invention of the cotton gin in the closing years of the last century gave extension to slavery, making it profitable to cultivate the new staple by enormous gangs of field hands working under the whip of the overseer in large plantations. Slavery became henceforth a business speculation in the States furthest south, and not, as in Old Virginia and Kentucky, a comparatively mild domestic system. The necessity of defending its peculiar institution against the attacks of a growing faction in the North compelled the South to throw all its intellectual strength into politics, which, for that matter, is the natural occupation and excitement of a social aristocracy. Meanwhile immigration sought the free States, and there was no middle class at the South. The "poor whites" were ignorant and degraded. There were people of education in the cities and on some of the plantations, but there was no great educated class from which a literature could proceed. And the culture of the South, such as it was, was becoming old-fashioned and local, as the section was isolated more and more from the rest of the Union and from the enlightened public opinion of Europe by its reactionary prejudices and its sensitiveness on the subject of slavery. Nothing can be imagined more ridiculously provincial than the sophomorical editorials in the southern press just before the outbreak of the war, or than the backward and ill-informed articles which passed for reviews in the poorly supported periodicals of the South.

In the general dearth of work of high and permanent value, one or two southern authors may be mentioned whose writings have at least done something to illustrate the life and scenery of their section. When in 1833 the Baltimore *Saturday Visiter* offered a prize of a hundred dollars for the best prose tale, one of the committee who awarded the prize to Poe's first story, the *MS. Found in a Bottle*, was John P. Kennedy, a Whig gentleman of Baltimore, who afterward became Secretary of the Navy in Fillmore's administration. The year before he had published *Swallow Barn*, a series of agreeable sketches of country life in Virginia. In 1835 and 1838 he published his two novels, *Horse-Shoe Robinson* and *Rob of the Bowl*, the former a story of the Revolutionary War in South Carolina; the latter an historical tale of colonial Maryland. These had sufficient success to warrant reprinting as late as 1852. But the most popular and voluminous of all Southern writers of fiction was William Gilmore Simms, a South Carolinian, who died in 1870. He wrote over thirty novels, mostly romances of Revolutionary history, southern life and wild adventure, among the best of which were the *Partisan*, 1835, and the *Yemassee*. Simms was an inferior Cooper, with a difference. His novels are good boys' books, but are crude and hasty in composition. He was strongly southern in his sympathies, though his newspaper, the *Charleston City Gazette*, took part against the Nullifiers. His miscellaneous writings include several histories and biographies, political tracts, addresses and critical papers contributed to southern magazines. He also wrote numerous poems, the most ambitious of which was *Atlantis, a Story of the Sea*, 1832. His poems have little value except as here and there illustrating local scenery and manners, as in *Southern Passages and Pictures*, 1839. Mr. John Esten Cooke's pleasant but not very strong *Virginia Comedians* was, perhaps, in literary quality the best southern novel produced before the civil war.

When Poe came to New York, the most conspicuous literary figure of the metropolis, with the possible exception of Bryant and Halleck, was N. P. Willis, one of the editors of the *Evening Mirror*, upon which journal Poe was for a time engaged. Willis had made a literary reputation, when a student at Yale, by his *Scripture Poems*, written in smooth blank verse. Afterward he had edited the *American Monthly* in his native city of Boston, and more recently he had published *Pencillings by the Way*, 1835, a pleasant record of European saunterings; *Inklings of Adventure*, 1836, a collection of dashing stories and sketches of American and foreign life; and *Letters from Under a Bridge*, 1839, a series of charming rural letters from his country place at Owego, on the Susquehanna. Willis's work, always graceful and sparkling, sometimes even brilliant, though light in substance and jaunty in style, had quickly raised him to the summit of popularity. During the years from 1835 to 1850 he was the most successful American magazinist, and even down to the day of his death, in 1867, he retained his hold upon the attention of the fashionable public by his easy paragraphing and correspondence in the *Mirror* and its successor, the *Home Journal*, which catered to the literary wants of the *beau monde*. Much of Willis's work was ephemeral, though clever of its kind, but a few of his best tales and sketches, such as *F. Smith, The Ghost Ball at Congress Hall, Edith Linsey*, and the *Lunatic's Skate*, together with some of the *Letters from Under a Bridge*, are worthy of preservation, not only as readable stories, but as society studies of life at American watering places like Nahant and Saratoga and Ballston Spa half a century ago. A number of his simpler poems, like *Unseen Spirits, Spring, To M—from Abroad*, and *Lines on Leaving Europe*, still retain a deserved place in collections and anthologies.

The senior editor of the *Mirror*, George P. Morris, was once a very popular song writer, and his *Woodman, Spare that Tree*, still survives. Other residents of New York City who have written single famous pieces were Clement C. Moore, a professor in the General Theological Seminary, whose *Visit from St. Nicholas*—" 'Twas the Night Before Christmas," etc.—is a favorite ballad in every nursery in the land; Charles Fenno Hoffman, a novelist of reputation in his time, but now remembered only as the author of the song, *Sparkling and Bright*, and the patriotic ballad of *Monterey;* Robert H. Messinger, a native of Boston, but long resident in New York, where he was a familiar figure in fashionable society, who wrote *Give Me the Old*, a fine ode with a choice Horatian flavor; and William Allen Butler, a lawyer and occasional writer, whose capital satire of *Nothing to Wear* was published anonymously and had a great run. Of younger poets, like Stoddard and Aldrich, who formerly wrote for the *Mirror* and who are still living and working in the maturity of their powers, it is not within the limits and design of this sketch to speak. But one of their contemporaries, Bayard Taylor, who died, American Minister at Berlin, in 1878, though a Pennsylvanian by birth and rearing, may be reckoned among the "literati of New York." A farmer lad from Chester County, who had learned the printer's trade and printed a little volume of his juvenile verses in 1844, he came to New York shortly after with credentials from Dr. Griswold, the editor of *Graham's*, and obtaining encouragement and aid from Willis, Horace Greeley and others, he set out to make the tour of Europe, walking from town to town in Germany and getting employment now and then at his trade to help pay the expenses of the trip. The story of these *Wanderjahre* he told in his *Views Afoot*, 1846. This was the first of eleven books of travel written during the course of his life. He was an inveterate nomad, and his journeyings carried him to the remotest regions—to California, India, China, Japan and the isles of the sea, to Central Africa and the Soudan, Palestine, Egypt, Iceland and the "byways of Europe." His head-quarters at home were in New York, where he did literary work for the *Tribune*. He was a rapid and incessant worker, throwing off many volumes of verse and prose, fiction, essays, sketches, translations and criticism, mainly contributed in the first instance to the magazines. His versatility was very marked, and his poetry ranged from *Rhymes of Travel*, 1848, and *Poems of the Orient*, 1854, to idyls and home ballads of Pennsylvania life, like the *Quaker Widow* and the *Old Pennsylvania Farmer*, and, on the other side, to ambitious and somewhat mystical poems, like the *Masque of the Gods*, 1872—written in four days—and dramatic experiments like the *Prophet*, 1874, and *Prince Deukalion*, 1878. He was a man of buoyant and eager nature, with a great appetite for new experience, a remarkable memory, a talent for learning languages, and a too great readiness to take the hue of his favorite books. From his facility, his openness to external impressions of scenery and costume and his habit of turning these at once into the service of his pen, it results that there is something "newspapery" and superficial about most of his prose. It is reporter's work, though reporting of a high order. His poetry, too, though full of glow and picturesqueness, is largely imitative, suggesting Tennyson not unfrequently, but more often Shelley. His spirited *Bedouin Song*, for example, has an echo of Shelley's *Lines to an Indian Air*:

> "From the desert I come to thee
> On a stallion shod with fire;
> And the winds are left behind
> In the speed of my desire.
> Under thy window I stand
> And the midnight hears my cry;
> I love thee, I love but thee
> With a love that shall not die."

The dangerous quickness with which he caught the manner of other poets made him an admirable parodist and translator. His *Echo Club*, 1876, contains some of the best travesties in the tongue, and his great translation of Goethe's *Faust*, 1870-71—with its wonderfully close reproduction of the original meters—is one of the glories of American literature. All in all, Taylor may unhesitatingly be put first among our poets of the second generation—the generation succeeding that of Longfellow and Lowell—although the lack in him of original genius self-determined to a peculiar sphere, or the want of an inward fixity and concentration to resist the rich tumult of outward impressions, has made him less significant in the history of our literary thought than some other writers less generously endowed.

Taylor's novels had the qualities of his verse. They were profuse, eloquent and faulty. *John Godfrey's Fortune*, 1864, gave a picture of bohemian life in New York. *Hannah Thurston*, 1863, and the *Story of Kennett*, 1866, introduced many incidents and persons from the old Quaker life of rural Pennsylvania, as Taylor remembered it in his boyhood. The former was like Hawthorne's *Blithedale Romance*, a satire on fanatics and reformers, and its heroine is a nobly conceived character, though drawn with some exaggeration. The *Story of Kennett*, which is largely autobiographic, has a greater freshness and reality than the others and is full of personal recollections. In these novels, as in his short stories, Taylor's pictorial skill is greater on the whole than his power of creating characters or inventing plots.

Literature in the West now began to have an existence. Another young poet from Chester County, Pa., namely, Thomas Buchanan Read, went to Cincinnati, and not to New York, to study sculpture and painting, about 1837, and one of his best-known poems, *Pons Maximus*, was written on the occasion of the opening of the suspension bridge across the Ohio. Read came East, to be sure, in 1841, and spent many years in our seaboard cities and in Italy. He was distinctly a minor poet, but some of his Pennsylvania pastorals, like the *Deserted Road*, have a natural sweetness; and his luxurious *Drifting*, which combines the methods of painting and poetry, is justly popular. *Sheridan's Ride*—perhaps his most current piece—is a rather forced production and has been over-praised. The two Ohio sister poets, Alice and Phœbe Cary, were attracted to New York in 1850, as soon as their literary success seemed assured. They made that city their home for the remainder of their lives. Poe praised Alice Cary's *Pictures of Memory*, and Phœbe's *Nearer Home* has become a favorite hymn. There is nothing peculiarly Western about the verse of the Cary sisters. It is the poetry of sentiment, memory, and domestic affection, entirely feminine, rather tame and diffuse as a whole, but tender and sweet, cherished by many good women and dear to simple hearts.

A stronger smack of the soil is in the negro melodies like *Uncle Ned, O Susanna, Old Folks at Home, Way Down South, Nelly was a Lady, My Old Kentucky Home*, etc., which were the work not of any southern poet, but of Stephen C. Foster, a native of Allegheny, Pa., and a resident of Cincinnati and Pittsburg. He composed the words and music of these, and many others of a similar kind, during the years 1847 to 1861. Taken together they form the most original and vital addition which this country has made to the psalmody of the world, and entitle Foster to the first rank among American song writers.

As Foster's plaintive melodies carried the pathos and humor of the plantation all over the land, so Mrs. Harriet Beecher Stowe's *Uncle Tom's Cabin*, 1852, brought home to millions of readers the sufferings of the negroes in the " black belt" of the cotton-growing States. This is the most popular novel ever written in America. Hundreds of thousands of copies were sold in this country and in England, and some forty translations were made into foreign tongues. In its dramatized form it still keeps the stage, and the statistics of circulating libraries show that even now it is in greater demand than any other single book. It did more than any other literary agency to rouse the public conscience to a sense of the shame and horror of slavery; more even than Garrison's *Liberator;* more than the indignant poems of Whittier and Lowell or the orations of Sumner and Phillips. It presented the thing concretely and dramatically, and in particular it made the odious Fugitive Slave Law forever impossible to enforce. It was useless for the defenders of slavery to protest that the picture was exaggerated and that overseers like Legree were the exception. The system under which such brutalities could happen, and did sometimes happen, was doomed. It is easy now to point out defects of taste and art in this masterpiece, to show that the tone is occasionally melodramatic, that some of the characters are conventional, and that the literary execution is in parts feeble and in others coarse. In spite of all it remains true that *Uncle Tom's Cabin* is a great book, the work of genius seizing instinctively upon its opportunity and uttering the thought of the time with a power that thrilled the heart of the nation and of the world. Mrs. Stowe never repeated her first success. Some of her novels of New England life, such as the *Minister's Wooing*, 1859, and the *Pearl of Orr's Island*, 1862, have a mild kind of interest, and contain truthful portraiture of provincial ways and traits; while later fictions of a domestic type, like *Pink and White Tyranny*, and *My Wife and I*, are really beneath criticism.

There were other Connecticut writers contemporary with Mrs. Stowe: Mrs. L. H. Sigourney, for example, a Hartford poetess, formerly known as "the Hemans of America," but now quite obsolete; and J. G. Percival, of New Haven, a shy and eccentric scholar, whose geological work was of value, and whose memory is preserved by one or two of his simpler poems, still in circulation, such as *To Seneca Lake* and the *Coral Grove*. Another Hartford poet, Brainard—already spoken of as an early friend of Whittier—died young, leaving a few pieces which show that his lyrical gift was spontaneous and genuine but had received little cultivation. A much younger writer than either of these, Donald G. Mitchell, of New Haven, has a more lasting place in our literature, by virtue of his charmingly written *Reveries of a Bachelor*,

1850, and *Dream Life*, 1852, stories which sketch themselves out in a series of reminiscences and lightly connected scenes, and which always appeal freshly to young men because they have that dreamy outlook upon life which is characteristic of youth. But, upon the whole, the most important contribution made by Connecticut in that generation to the literary stock of America was the Beecher family. Lyman Beecher had been an influential preacher and theologian, and a sturdy defender of orthodoxy against Boston Unitarianism. Of his numerous sons and daughters, all more or less noted for intellectual vigor and independence, the most eminent were Mrs. Stowe and Henry Ward Beecher, the great pulpit orator of Brooklyn. Mr. Beecher was too busy a man to give more than his spare moments to general literature. His sermons, lectures, and addresses were reported for the daily papers and printed in part in book form; but these lose greatly when divorced from the large, warm, and benignant personality of the man. His volumes made up of articles in the *Independent* and the *Ledger*, such as *Star Papers*, 1855, and *Eyes and Ears*, 1862, contain many delightful *morceaux* upon country life and similar topics, though they are hardly wrought with sufficient closeness and care to take a permanent place in letters. Like Willis's *Ephemeræ*, they are excellent literary journalism, but hardly literature.

We may close our retrospect of American literature before 1861 with a brief notice of one of the most striking literary phenomena of the time— the *Leaves of Grass* of Walt Whitman, published at Brooklyn in 1855. The author, born at West Hills, Long Island, in 1819, had been printer, school-teacher, editor, and builder. He had scribbled a good deal of poetry of the ordinary kind, which attracted little attention, but finding conventional rhymes and meters too cramping a vehicle for his need of expression, he discarded them for a kind of rhythmic chant, of which the following is a fair specimen:

"Press close, bare bosom'd night! Press close, magnetic,
    nourishing night!
Night of south winds! night of the few large stars!
Still, nodding night! mad, naked, summer night!"

The invention was not altogether a new one. The English translation of the Psalms of David and of some of the Prophets, the *Poems of Ossian*, and some of Matthew Arnold's unrhymed pieces, especially the *Strayed Reveller*, have an irregular rhythm of this kind, to say nothing of the old Anglo-Saxon poems, like *Beowulf*, and the Scripture paraphrases attributed to Cædmon. But this species of *oratio soluta*, carried to the lengths to which Whitman carried it, had an air of novelty which was displeasing to some, while to others, weary of familiar measures and jingling rhymes, it was refreshing in its boldness and freedom. There is no consenting estimate of this poet.

Many think that his so-called poems are not poems at all, but simply a bad variety of prose; that there is nothing to him beyond a combination of affectation and indecency; and that the Whitman *culte* is a passing "fad" of a few literary men, and especially of a number of English critics like Rossetti, Swinburne, Buchanan, etc., who, being determined to have something unmistakably American —that is, different from any thing else—in writings from this side of the water before they will acknowledge any originality in them, have been misled into discovering in Whitman "the poet of Democracy." Others maintain that he is the greatest of American poets, or, indeed, of all modern poets; that he is "cosmic," or universal, and that he has put an end forever to puling rhymes and lines chopped up into metrical feet. Whether Whitman's poetry is formally poetry at all or merely the raw material of poetry, the chaotic and amorphous impression which it makes on readers of conservative tastes results from his effort to take up into his verse elements which poetry has usually left out — the ugly, the earthy, and even the disgusting; the "under side of things," which he holds not to be prosaic when apprehended with a strong, masculine joy in life and nature seen in all their aspects. The lack of these elements in the conventional poets seems to him and his disciples like leaving out the salt from the ocean, making poetry merely pretty and blinking whole classes of facts. Hence the naturalism and animalism of some of the divisions in *Leaves of Grass*, particularly that entitled *Children of Adam*, which gave great offense by its immodesty, or its outspokenness. Whitman holds that nakedness is chaste; that all the functions of the body in healthy exercise are equally clean; that all, in fact, are divine, and that matter is as divine as spirit. The effort to get every thing into his poetry, to speak out his thought just as it comes to him, accounts, too, for his way of cataloguing objects without selection. His single expressions are often unsurpassed for descriptive beauty and truth. He speaks of "the vitreous pour of the full moon, just tinged with blue," of the "lisp" of the plane, of the prairies, "where herds of buffalo make a crawling spread of the square miles." But if there is any eternal distinction between poetry and prose the most liberal canons of the poetic art will never agree to accept lines like these:

"And [I] remember putting plasters on the galls of his neck and ankles;
He stayed with me a week before he was recuperated, and passed north."

Whitman is the spokesman of Democracy and of the future; full of brotherliness and hope, loving the warm, gregarious pressure of the crowd and the touch of his comrade's elbow in the ranks. He liked the people—multitudes of people; the swarm of life beheld from a Broadway omnibus or a Brooklyn ferry-boat. The rowdy and the Negro truck-driver were closer to his sympathy than the gentleman and the scholar. "I loafe and invite my soul," he writes: "I sound my barbaric yawp over the roofs of the world." His poem *Walt Whitman*, frankly egotistic, simply describes himself as a typical, average man—the same as any other man, and therefore not individual but universal. He has great tenderness and heartiness— "the good gray poet;" and during the civil war he devoted himself unreservedly to the wounded soldiers in the Washington hospitals—an experience which he has related in the *Dresser* and elsewhere. It is characteristic of his rough and ready *camaraderie* to use slang and newspaper English in his poetry, to call himself Walt instead of Walter, and to have his picture taken in a slouch hat and with a flannel shirt open at the throat. His decriers allege that he poses for effect; that he is simply a backward eddy in the tide, and significant only as a temporary reaction against ultra civilization—like Thoreau, though in a different way. But with all his mistakes in art there is a healthy, virile, tumultuous pulse of life in his lyric utterance and a great sweep of imagination in his panoramic view of times and countries. One likes to read him because he feels so good, enjoys so fully the play of his senses, and has such a lusty confidence in his own immortality and in the prospects of the human race. Stripped of verbiage and repetition, his ideas are not many. His indebtedness to Emerson—who wrote an introduction to the *Leaves of Grass*—is manifest. He sings of man and not men, and the individual differences of character, sentiment, and passion, the *dramatic* elements of life, find small place in his system. It is too early to say what will be his final position in literary history. But it is noteworthy that the democratic masses have not accepted him yet as their poet. Whittier and Longfellow, the poets of conscience and feeling, are the darlings of the American people. The admiration, and even the knowledge of Whitman, are mostly esoteric, confined to the literary class. It is also not without significance as to the ultimate reception of his innovations in verse that he has numerous parodists, but no imitators. The tendency among our younger poets is not toward the abandonment of rhyme and meter, but toward the introduction of new stanza forms and an increasing carefulness and finish in the *technique* of their art. It is observable, too, that in his most inspired passages Whitman reverts to the old forms of verse; to blank verse, for example, in the *Man-of-War-Bird*:

> "Thou who hast slept all night upon the storm,
> Waking renewed on thy prodigious pinions," etc.,

and elsewhere not infrequently to dactylic hexameters and pentameters:

> "Earth of shine and dark, mottling the tide of the river! . . .
> Far-swooping, elbowed earth! rich, apple-blossomed earth."

Indeed, Whitman's most popular poem, *My Captain*, written after the assassination of Abraham Lincoln, differs little in form from ordinary verse, as a stanza of it will show:

"My captain does not answer, his lips are pale and still;
My father does not feel my arm, he has no pulse nor will;
The ship is anchored safe and sound, its voyage closed and done;
From fearful trip the victor ship comes in with object won.
    Exult, O shores, and ring, O bells!
    But I, with mournful tread,
    Walk the deck, my captain lies
    Fallen, cold and dead."

This is from *Drum Taps*, a volume of poems of the civil war. Whitman has also written prose having much the same quality as his poetry: *Democratic Vistas*, *Memoranda of the Civil War*, and more recently, *Specimen Days*. His residence of late years has been at Camden, New Jersey, where a centennial edition of his writings was published in 1876.

1. William Cullen Bryant. Thanatopsis. To a Waterfowl. Green River. Hymn to the North Star. A Forest Hymn. "O Fairest of the Rural Maids." June. The Death of the Flowers. The Evening Wind. The Battle Field. The Planting of the Apple-tree. The Flood of Years.

2. John Greenleaf Whittier. Cassandra South-

wick. The New Wife and the Old. The Virginia Slave Mother. Randolph of Roanoke. Barclay of Ary. The Witch of Wenham. Skipper Ireson's Ride. Marguerite. Maud Muller. Telling the Bees. My Playmate. Barbara Frietchie. Ichabod. Laus Deo. Snow Bound.

3. Edgar Allan Poe. The Raven. The Bells. Israfel. Ulalume. To Helen. The City in the Sea. Annabel Lee. To One in Paradise. The Sleeper. The Valley of Unrest. The Fall of the House of Usher. Ligeia. William Wilson. The Cask of Amontillado. The Assignation. The Masque of the Red Death. Narrative of A. Gordon Pym.

4. N. P. Willis. Select Prose Writings. New York: Charles Scribner's Sons. 1886.

5. Mrs. H. B. Stowe. Uncle Tom's Cabin. Oldtown Folks.

6. W. G. Simms. The Partisan. The Yemassee.

7. Bayard Taylor. A Bacchic Ode. Hylas. Kubleh. The Soldier and the Pard. Sicilian Wine. Taurus. Serapion. The Metempsychosis of the Pine. The Temptation of Hassan Ben Khaled. Bedouin Song. Euphorion. The Quaker Widow. John Reid. Lars. Views Afoot. By-ways of Europe. The Story of Kennett. The Echo Club.

8. Walt Whitman. My Captain. "When Lilacs Last in the Door-yard Bloomed." "Out of the Cradle Endlessly Rocking." Pioneers, O Pi-

oneers. The Mystic Trumpeter. A Woman at Auction. Sea-shore Memoirs. Passage to India. Mannahatta. The Wound Dresser. Longings for Home.

9. Poets of America. By E. C. Stedman. Boston: Houghton, Mifflin & Co. 1885.

CHAPTER VII.

LITERATURE SINCE 1861.

A GENERATION has nearly passed since the outbreak of the civil war, and although public affairs are still mainly in the hands of men who had reached manhood before the conflict opened, or who were old enough at that time to remember clearly its stirring events, the younger men who are daily coming forward to take their places know it only by tradition. It makes a definite break in the history of our literature, and a number of new literary schools and tendencies have appeared since its close. As to the literature of the war itself, it was largely the work of writers who had already reached or passed middle age. All of the more important authors described in the last three chapters survived the Rebellion, except Poe, who died in 1849, Prescott, who died in 1859, and Thoreau and Hawthorne, who died in the second and fourth years of the war, respectively. The final and authoritative history of the struggle has not yet been written, and cannot be written for many years to come. Many partial and tentative accounts have, however, appeared, among which may be mentioned, on the northern side,

Horace Greeley's *American Conflict*, 1864-66; Vice-president Wilson's *Rise and Fall of the Slave Power in America*, and J. W. Draper's *American Civil War*, 1868-70; on the southern side Alexander H. Stephens's *Confederate States of America*, Jefferson Davis's *Rise and Fall of the Confederate States of America*, and E. A. Pollard's *Lost Cause*. These, with the exception of Dr. Draper's philosophical narrative, have the advantage of being the work of actors in the political or military events which they describe, and the disadvantage of being, therefore, partisan—in some instances passionately partisan. A storehouse of materials for the coming historian is also at hand in Frank Moore's great collection, the *Rebellion Record;* in numerous regimental histories and histories of special armies, departments, and battles, like W. Swinton's *Army of the Potomac;* in the autobiographies and recollections of Grant and Sherman and other military leaders; in the "war papers," now publishing in the *Century* magazine, and in innumerable sketches and reminiscences by officers and privates on both sides.

The war had its poetry, its humors and its general literature, some of which have been mentioned in connection with Whittier, Lowell, Holmes, Whitman, and others; and some of which remain to be mentioned, as the work of new writers, or of writers who had previously made little mark. There were war songs on both sides, few of which had much literary value excepting, perhaps, James

R. Randall's southern ballad, *Maryland, My Maryland*, sung to the old college air of *Lauriger Horatius*, and the grand martial chorus of *John Brown's Body*, an old Methodist hymn, to which the northern armies beat time as they went "marching on." Randall's song, though spirited, was marred by its fire-eating absurdities about "vandals" and "minions" and "northern scum," the cheap insults of the southern newspaper press. To furnish the *John Brown* chorus with words worthy of the music, Mrs. Julia Ward Howe wrote her *Battle Hymn of the Republic*, a noble poem, but rather too fine and literary for a song, and so never fully accepted by the soldiers. Among the many verses which voiced the anguish and the patriotism of that stern time, which told of partings and homecomings, of women waiting by desolate hearths, in country homes, for tidings of husbands and sons who had gone to the war, or which celebrated individual deeds of heroism or sang the thousand private tragedies and heart-breaks of the great conflict, by far the greater number were of too humble a grade to survive the feeling of the hour. Among the best or the most popular of them were Kate Putnam Osgood's *Driving Home the Cows*, Mrs. Ethel Lynn Beers's *All Quiet Along the Potomac*, Forceythe Willson's *Old Sergeant*, and John James Piatt's *Riding to Vote*. Of the poets whom the war brought out, or developed, the most noteworthy were Henry Timrod, of South Carolina, and Henry Howard Brownell, of Connecticut. During the war Timrod was with the Confederate Army of the West, as correspondent for the *Charleston Mercury*, and in 1864 he became assistant editor of the *South Carolinian*, at Columbia. Sherman's "march to the sea" broke up his business, and he returned to Charleston. A complete edition of his poems was published in 1873, six years after his death. The prettiest of all Timrod's poems is *Katie*, but more to our present purpose are *Charleston*—written in the time of blockade—and the *Unknown Dead*, which tells

> "Of nameless graves on battle plains,
> Wash'd by a single winter's rains,
> Where, some beneath Virginian hills,
> And some by green Atlantic rills,
> Some by the waters of the West,
> A myriad unknown heroes rest."

When the war was over a poet of New York State, F. M. Finch, sang of these and of other graves in his beautiful Decoration Day lyric, *The Blue and the Gray*, which spoke the word of reconciliation and consecration for North and South alike.

Brownell, whose *Lyrics of a Day* and *War Lyrics* were published respectively in 1864 and 1866, was private secretary to Farragut, on whose flag-ship, the *Hartford*, he was present at several great naval engagements, such as the "Passage of the Forts" below New Orleans, and the action off Mobile, described in his poem, the *Bay Fight*.

With some roughness and unevenness of execution, Brownell's poetry had a fire which places him next to Whittier as the Körner of the civil war. In him, especially, as in Whittier, is that Puritan sense of the righteousness of his cause which made the battle for the Union a holy war to the crusaders against slavery:

> " Full red the furnace fires must glow
> That melt the ore of mortal kind :
> The mills of God are grinding slow,
> But ah, how close they grind!
>
> " To-day the Dahlgren and the drum
> Are dread apostles of his name;
> His kingdom here can only come
> By chrism of blood and flame."

One of the earliest martyrs of the war was Theodore Winthrop, hardly known as a writer until the publication in the *Atlantic Monthly* of his vivid sketches of *Washington as a Camp*, describing the march of his regiment, the famous New York Seventh, and its first quarters in the Capitol at Washington. A tragic interest was given to these papers by Winthrop's gallant death in the action of Big Bethel, June 10, 1861. While this was still fresh in public recollection his manuscript novels were published, together with a collection of his stories and sketches reprinted from the magazines. His novels, though in parts crude and immature, have a dash and buoyancy—an out-door air about them—which give the reader a winning impression

LITERATURE SINCE 1861.   245

of Winthrop's personality. The best of them is, perhaps, *Cecil Dreeme*, a romance that reminds one a little of Hawthorne, and the scene of which is the New York University building on Washington Square, a locality that has been further celebrated in Henry James's novel of *Washington Square*.

Another member of this same Seventh Regiment, Fitz James O'Brien, an Irishman by birth, who died at Baltimore, in 1862, from the effects of a wound received in a cavalry skirmish, had contributed to the magazines a number of poems and of brilliant though fantastic tales, among which the *Diamond Lens* and *What Was It?* had something of Edgar A. Poe's quality. Another Irish-American, Charles G. Halpine, under the pen-name of "Miles O'Reilly," wrote a good many clever ballads of the war, partly serious and partly in comic brogue. Prose writers of note furnished the magazines with narratives of their experience at the seat of war, among papers of which kind may be mentioned Dr. Holmes's *My Search for the Captain*, in the *Atlantic Monthly*, and Colonel T. W. Higginson's *Army Life in a Black Regiment*, collected into a volume in 1870.

Of the public oratory of the war the foremost example is the ever-memorable address of Abraham Lincoln at the dedication of the National Cemetery at Gettysburg. The war had brought the nation to its intellectual majority. In the stress of that terrible fight there was no room for buncombe and verbiage, such as the newspapers and stump-speakers used to dole out in *ante bellum* days. Lincoln's speech is short—a few grave words which he turned aside for a moment to speak in the midst of his task of saving the country. The speech is simple, naked of figures, every sentence impressed with a sense of responsibility for the work yet to be done and with a stern determination to do it. "In a larger sense," it says, "we cannot dedicate, we cannot consecrate, we cannot hallow this ground. The brave men, living and dead, who struggled here have consecrated it far above our poor power to add or detract. The world will little note nor long remember what we say here, but it can never forget what they did here. It is for us, the living, rather to be dedicated here to the unfinished work which they who fought here have thus far so nobly advanced. It is rather for us to be here dedicated to the great task remaining before us; that from these honored dead we take increased devotion to that cause for which they gave the last full measure of devotion; that we here highly resolve that these dead shall not have died in vain: that this nation, under God, shall have a new birth of freedom; and that government of the people, by the people, for the people, shall not perish from the earth." Here was eloquence of a different sort from the sonorous perorations of Webster or the polished climaxes of Everett. As we read the plain, strong language of this brief classic, with its solemnity, its restraint, its "brave old wisdom of sincerity," we seem to see the president's homely features irradiated with the light of coming martyrdom—

> " The kindly-earnest, brave, foreseeing man,
> Sagacious, patient, dreading praise, not blame,
> New birth of our new soil, the first American."

Within the past quarter of a century the popular school of American humor has reached its culmination. Every man of genius who is a humorist at all is so in a way peculiar to himself. There is no lack of individuality in the humor of Irving and Hawthorne and the wit of Holmes and Lowell, but although they are new in subject and application they are not new in kind. Irving, as we have seen, was the literary descendant of Addison. The character sketches in *Bracebridge Hall* are of the same family with Sir Roger de Coverley and the other figures of the Spectator Club. *Knickerbocker's History of New York*, though purely American in its matter, is not distinctly American in its method, which is akin to the mock heroic of Fielding and the irony of Swift in the *Voyage to Lilliput*. Irving's humor, like that of all the great English humorists, had its root in the perception of character—of the characteristic traits of men and classes of men, as ground of amusement. It depended for its effect, therefore, upon its truthfulness, its dramatic insight and sympathy, as did the humor of Shakspere, of Sterne, Lamb, and Thackeray. This perception of the characteristic, when pushed to excess, issues in grotesque and caricature, as in some of Dickens's inferior creations, which are little more than personified single tricks of manner, speech, feature, or dress. Hawthorne's rare humor differed from Irving's in temper but not in substance, and belonged, like Irving's, to the English variety. Dr. Holmes's more pronouncedly comic verse does not differ specifically from the *facetiæ* of Thomas Hood, but his prominent trait is wit, which is the laughter of the head as humor is of the heart. The same is true, with qualifications, of Lowell, whose *Biglow Papers*, though humor of an original sort in their revelation of Yankee character, are essentially satirical. It is the cleverness, the shrewdness of the hits in the *Biglow Papers*, their logical, that is, *witty* character, as distinguished from their drollery, that arrests the attention. They are funny, but they are not so funny as they are smart. In all these writers humor was blent with more serious qualities, which gave fineness and literary value to their humorous writings. Their view of life was not exclusively comic. But there has been a class of jesters, of professional humorists in America, whose product is so indigenous, so different, if not in essence, yet at least in form and expression, from any European humor, that it may be regarded as a unique addition to the comic literature of the world. It has been accepted as such in England, where Artemus Ward and Mark Twain are familiar to multitudes who have never read the *One-Hoss-Shay* or the *Courtin'*. And though it would be ridiculous to maintain that either of these writers takes rank with Lowell and Holmes, or to deny that there is an amount of flatness and coarseness in many of their labored fooleries which puts large portions of their writings below the line where real literature begins, still it will not do to ignore them as mere buffoons, or even to predict that their humors will soon be forgotten. It is true that no literary fashion is more subject to change than the fashion of a jest, and that jokes that make one generation laugh seem insipid to the next. But there is something perennial in the fun of Rabelais, whom Bacon called "the great jester of France;" and though the puns of Shakspere's clowns are detestable the clowns themselves have not lost their power to amuse.

The Americans are not a gay people, but they are fond of a joke. Lincoln's "little stories" were characteristically Western, and it is doubtful whether he was more endeared to the masses by his solid virtues than by the humorous perception which made him one of them. The humor of which we are speaking now is a strictly popular and national possession. Though America has never, or not until lately, had a comic paper ranking with *Punch* or *Charivari* or the *Fliegende Blätter*, every newspaper has had its funny column. Our humorists have been graduated from the journalist's desk and sometimes from the printing-press, and now and then a local or country newspaper has risen into sudden prosperity from the possession of a new humorist, as in the case of G. D. Prentice's *Courier-Journal*, or more recently of the *Cleveland Plain Dealer*, the *Danbury News*, the *Burlington Hawkeye*, the *Arkansaw Traveller*, the *Texas Siftings* and numerous others. Nowadays there are even syndicates of humorists, who co-operate to supply fun for certain groups of periodicals. Of course the great majority of these manufacturers of jests for newspapers and comic almanacs are doomed to swift oblivion. But it is not so certain that the best of the class, like Clemens and Browne, will not long continue to be read as illustrative of one side of the American mind, or that their best things will not survive as long as the *mots* of Sydney Smith, which are still as current as ever. One of the earliest of them was Seba Smith, who, under the name of Major Jack Downing, did his best to make Jackson's administration ridiculous. B. P. Shillaber's "Mrs. Partington"—a sort of American Mrs. Malaprop—enjoyed great vogue before the war. Of a somewhat higher kind were the *Phœnixiana*, 1855, and *Squibob Papers*, 1856, of Lieutenant George H. Derby, "John Phœnix," one of the pioneers of literature on the Pacific coast at the time of the California gold fever of '49. Derby's proposal for *A New System of English Grammar*, his satirical account of the topographical survey of the two miles of road between San Francisco and the Mission Dolores, and his picture gallery made out of the conventional houses, steam-boats, rail-cars, runaway negroes and other designs which used to figure in the advertising columns of the newspapers, were all very ingenious and clever. But all these pale before Artemus Ward—"Artemus the delicious," as Charles Reade called him—who first secured for this peculiarly American type of humor a hearing and reception abroad. Ever since the invention of Hosea Biglow, an imaginary personage of some sort, under cover of whom the author might conceal his own identity, has seemed a necessity to our humorists. Artemus Ward was a traveling showman who went about the country exhibiting a collection of wax "figgers" and whose experiences and reflections were reported in grammar and spelling of a most ingeniously eccentric kind. His inventor was Charles F. Browne, originally of Maine, a printer by trade and afterward a newspaper writer and editor at Boston, Toledo and Cleveland, where his comicalities in the *Plaindealer* first began to attract notice. In 1860 he came to New York and joined the staff of *Vanity Fair*, a comic weekly of much brightness, which ran a short career and perished for want of capital. When Browne began to appear as a public lecturer people who had formed an idea of him from his impersonation of the shrewd and vulgar old showman were surprised to find him a gentlemanly-looking young man, who came upon the platform in correct evening dress, and "spoke his piece" in a quiet and somewhat mournful manner, stopping in apparent surprise when any one in the audience laughed at any uncommonly outrageous absurdity. In London, where he delivered his *Lecture on the Mormons*, in 1866, the gravity of his bearing at first imposed upon his hearers, who had come to the hall in search of instructive information and were disappointed at the inadequate nature of the panorama which Browne had had made to illustrate his lecture. Occasionally some hitch would occur in the machinery of this and the lecturer would leave the rostrum for a few moments to "work the moon" that shone upon the Great Salt Lake, apologizing on his return on the ground that he was "a man short" and offering "to pay a good salary to any respectable boy of good parentage and education who is a good moonist." When it gradually dawned upon the British intellect that these and similar devices of the lecturer—such as the soft music which he had the pianist play at pathetic passages—nay, that the panorama and even the lecture itself were of a humorous intention, the joke began to take, and Artemus's success in England became assured. He was employed as one of the editors of *Punch*, but died at Southampton in the year following.

Some of Artemus Ward's effects were produced by cacography or bad spelling, but there was genius in the wildly erratic way in which he handled even this rather low order of humor. It is a curious commentary on the wretchedness of our English orthography that the phonetic spelling of a word, as for example, *wuz* for *was*, should be in itself an occasion of mirth. Other verbal effects of a different kind were among his devices, as in the passage where the seventeen widows of a deceased Mormon offered themselves to Artemus.

"And I said, 'Why is this thus? What is the reason of this thusness?' They hove a sigh— seventeen sighs of different size. They said—

"'O, soon thou will be gonested away.'

"I told them that when I got ready to leave a place I wentested.'

"They said, 'Doth not like us?'

"I said, 'I doth—I doth.'

"I also said, 'I hope your intentions are honorable, as I am a lone child—my parents being far—far away.'

"They then said, 'Wilt not marry us?'

"I said, 'O no, it cannot was.'

"When they cried, 'O cruel man! this is too much!—O! too much,' I told them that it was on account of the muchness that I declined."

It is hard to define the difference between the humor of one writer and another, or of one nation and another. It can be felt and can be illustrated by quoting examples, but scarcely described in general terms. It has been said of that class of American humorists of which Artemus Ward is a representative that their peculiarity consists in extravagance, surprise, audacity and irreverence. But all these qualities have characterized other schools of humor. There is the same element of surprise in De Quincey's anticlimax, " Many a man has dated his ruin from some murder or other which, perhaps, at the time he thought little of," as in Artemus's truism that "a comic paper ought to publish a joke now and then." The violation of logic which makes us laugh at an Irish bull is likewise the source of the humor in Artemus's saying of Jeff Davis, that "it would have been better than ten dollars in his pocket if he had never been born." Or in his advice, "Always live within your income, even if you have to borrow money to do so;" or, again, in his announcement that, " Mr. Ward will pay no debts of his own contracting." A kind of ludicrous confusion, caused by an unusual collocation of words, is also one of his favorite tricks, as when he says of Brigham Young, " He's the most married man I ever saw in my life;" or when, having been drafted at several hundred different places where he had been exhibiting his wax figures, he says that if he went on he should soon become a regiment, and adds, "I never knew that there was so many of me." With this a whimsical under-statement and an affectation of simplicity, as where he expresses his willingness to sacrifice "even his wife's relations" on the altar of patriotism; or, where, in delightful unconsciousness of his own sins against orthography, he pronounces that " Chaucer was a great poet, but he couldn't spell," or where he says of the feast of raw dog, tendered him by the Indian chief, Wocky-bocky, " It don't agree with me. I prefer simple food." On the whole, it may be said of original humor of this kind, as of other forms of originality in literature, that the elements of it are old, but their combinations are novel. Other humorists, like Henry W. Shaw ("Josh Billings"), and David R. Locke, ("Petroleum V. Nasby"), have used bad spelling as a part of their machinery; while Robert H. Newell, ("Orpheus C. Kerr"), Samuel L. Clemens, ("Mark Twain"), and more recently "Bill Nye," though belonging to the same school of low or broad comedy, have discarded cacography. Of these the most eminent, by all odds, is Mark Twain, who has probably made more people laugh than any other living writer. A Missourian by birth (1835), he served the usual apprenticeship at type-setting and editing country newspapers; spent seven years as a pilot on a Mississippi steam-boat, and seven years more mining and journalizing in Nevada, where he conducted the Virginia City *Enterprise*; finally drifted to San Francisco, and was associated with Bret Harte on the *Californian*, and in 1867 published his first book, the *Jumping Frog*. This was succeeded by the *Innocents Abroad*, 1869; *Roughing It*, 1872; *A Tramp Abroad*, 1880, and by others not so good.

Mark Twain's drolleries have frequently the same air of innocence and surprise as Artemus Ward's, and there is a like suddenness in his turns of expression, as where he speaks of "the calm confidence of a Christian with four aces." If he did not originate, he at any rate employed very effectively that now familiar device of the newspaper "funny man," of putting a painful situation euphemistically, as when he says of a man who was hanged that he "received injuries which terminated in his death." He uses to the full extent the American humorist's favorite resources of exaggeration and irreverence. An instance of the former quality may be seen in his famous description of a dog chasing a coyote, in *Roughing It*, or in his interview with the lightning-rod agent in *Mark Twain's Sketches*, 1875. He is a shrewd observer, and his humor has a more satirical side than Artemus Ward's, sometimes passing into downright denunciation. He delights particularly in ridiculing sentimental humbug and moralizing cant. He runs a tilt, as has been said, at "copy-book texts," at the temperance reformer, the tract distributor, the Good Boy of Sunday-school literature, and the women who send bouquets and sympathetic letters to interesting criminals. He gives a ludicrous turn to famous historical anecdotes, such as the story of George Washington and his little hatchet; burlesques the time-honored adventure, in nautical romances, of the starving crew casting lots in the long boat, and spoils the dignity of antiquity by modern trivialities, saying of a discontented sailor on Columbus's ship, "He wanted fresh shad." The fun of *Innocents Abroad* consists in this irreverent application of modern, common sense, utilitarian, democratic standards to the memorable places and historic associations of

Europe. Tried by this test the Old Masters in the picture galleries become laughable. Abelard was a precious scoundrel, and the raptures of the guide books are parodied without mercy. The tourist weeps at the grave of Adam. At Genoa he drives the *cicerone* to despair by pretending never to have heard of Christopher Columbus, and inquiring innocently, "Is he dead?" It is Europe vulgarized and stripped of its illusions—Europe seen by a Western newspaper reporter without any "historic imagination."

The method of this whole class of humorists is the opposite of Addison's or Irving's or Thackeray's. It does not amuse by the perception of the characteristic. It is not founded upon truth, but upon incongruity, distortion, unexpectedness. Every thing in life is reversed, as in opera bouffe, and turned topsy turvy, so that paradox takes the place of the natural order of things. Nevertheless they have supplied a wholesome criticism upon sentimental excesses, and the world is in their debt for many a hearty laugh.

In the *Atlantic Monthly* for December, 1863, appeared a tale entitled the *Man Without a Country*, which made a great sensation, and did much to strengthen patriotic feeling in one of the darkest hours of the nation's history. It was the story of one Philip Nolan, an army officer, whose head had been turned by Aaron Burr, and who, having been censured by a court-martial for some minor offense, exclaimed, petulantly, upon mention being made of the United States Government, "Damn the United States! I wish that I might never hear the United States mentioned again." Thereupon he was sentenced to have his wish, and was kept all his life aboard the vessels of the navy, being sent off on long voyages and transferred from ship to ship, with orders to those in charge that his country and its concerns should never be spoken of in his presence. Such an air of reality was given to the narrative by incidental references to actual persons and occurrences that many believed it true, and some were found who remembered Philip Nolan, but had heard different versions of his career. The author of this clever hoax—if hoax it may be called—was Edward Everett Hale, a Unitarian clergyman of Boston, who published a collection of stories in 1868, under the fantastic title, *If, Yes, and Perhaps*, indicating thereby that some of the tales were possible, some of them probable, and others might even be regarded as essentially true. A similar collection, *His Level Best and Other Stories* was published in 1873, and in the interval three volumes of a somewhat different kind, the *Ingham Papers* and *Sybaris and Other Homes*, both in 1869, and *Ten Times One Is Ten*, in 1871. The author shelters himself behind the imaginary figure of Captain Frederic Ingham, pastor of the Sandemanian Church at Naguadavick, and the same characters have a way of re-appearing in his successive volumes as old friends of the reader, which is pleasant at first, but in the end a little tiresome. Mr. Hale is one of the most original and ingenious of American story writers. The old device of making wildly improbable inventions appear like fact by a realistic treatment of details — a device employed by Swift and Edgar Poe, and more lately by Jules Verne — became quite fresh and novel in his hands, and was managed with a humor all his own. Some of his best stories are *My Double and How He Undid Me*, describing how a busy clergyman found an Irishman who looked so much like himself that he trained him to pass as his duplicate, and sent him to do duty in his stead at public meetings, dinners, etc., thereby escaping bores and getting time for real work; the *Brick Moon*, a story of a projectile built and launched into space, to revolve in a fixed meridian about the earth and serve mariners as a mark of longitude; the *Rag Man and Rag Woman*, a tale of an impoverished couple who made a competence by saving the pamphlets, advertisements, wedding cards, etc., that came to them through the mail, and developing a paper business on that basis; and the *Skeleton in the Closet*, which shows how the fate of the Southern Confederacy was involved in the adventures of a certain hoop-skirt, "built in the eclipse and rigged with curses dark." Mr. Hale's historical scholarship and his exact habit of mind have aided him in the art of giving *vraisemblance* to absurdities. He is known in philanthropy as well as in letters, and his tales have a cheerful, busy, practical way with them in consonance with his motto, "Look up and not down, look forward and not back, look out and not in, and lend a hand."

It is too soon to sum up the literary history of the last quarter of a century. The writers who have given it shape are still writing, and their work is therefore incomplete. But on the slightest review of it two facts become manifest: first, that New England has lost its long monopoly; and, secondly, that a marked feature of the period is the growth of realistic fiction. The electric tension of the atmosphere for thirty years preceding the civil war, the storm and stress of great public contests, and the intellectual stir produced by transcendentalism seem to have been more favorable to poetry and literary idealism than present conditions are. At all events there are no new poets who rank with Whittier, Longfellow, Lowell, and others of the elder generation, although George H. Boker, in Philadelphia, R. H. Stoddard and E. C. Stedman, in New York, and T. B. Aldrich, first in New York and afterward in Boston, have written creditable verse; not to speak of younger writers, whose work, however, for the most part, has been more distinguished by delicacy of execution than by native impulse. Mention has been made of the establishment of *Harper's Monthly Magazine*, which, under the conduct of its accomplished editor, George W. Curtis, has provided the public with an abundance of good reading. The old *Putnam's Monthly*, which ran from 1853 to 1858, and had a strong corps of contributors, was revived in 1868, and continued by that name till 1870, when it was succeeded by *Scribner's Monthly*, under the editorship of Dr. J. G. Holland, and this in 1881 by the *Century*, an efficient rival of *Harper's* in circulation, in literary excellence, and in the beauty of its wood engraving, the American school of which art these two great periodicals have done much to develop and encourage. Another New York monthly, the *Galaxy*, ran from 1866 to 1878, and was edited by Richard Grant White. During the present year a new *Scribner's Magazine* has also taken the field. The *Atlantic*, in Boston, and *Lippincott's*, in Philadelphia, are no unworthy competitors with these for public favor.

During the forties began a new era of national expansion, somewhat resembling that described in a former chapter, and, like that, bearing fruit eventually in literature. The cession of Florida to the United States in 1845, and the annexation of Texas in the same year, were followed by the purchase of California in 1847, and its admission as a State in 1850. In 1849 came the great rush to the California gold fields. San Francisco, at first a mere collection of tents and board shanties, with a few adobe huts, grew with incredible rapidity into a great city; the wicked and wonderful city apostrophized by Bret Harte in his poem, *San Francisco:*

"Serene, indifferent of Fate,
Thou sittest at the Western Gate;
Upon thy heights so lately won
Still slant the banners of the sun. . . .
I know thy cunning and thy greed,
Thy hard, high lust and willful deed."

The adventurers of all lands and races who flocked to the Pacific coast found there a motley state of society between civilization and savagery. There were the relics of the old Mexican occupation, the Spanish missions, with their Christianized Indians; the wild tribes of the plains—Apaches, Utes, and Navajoes; the Chinese coolies and washermen, all elements strange to the Atlantic seaboard and the States of the interior. The gold-hunters crossed, in stages or caravans, enormous prairies, alkaline deserts dotted with sage brush and seamed by deep cañons, and passes through gigantic mountain ranges. On the coast itself nature was unfamiliar: the climate was sub-tropical; fruits and vegetables grew to a mammoth size, corresponding to the enormous redwoods in the Mariposa groves and the prodigious scale of the scenery in the valley of the Yo Semite and the snow-capped peaks of the Sierras. At first there were few women, and the men led a wild, lawless existence in the mining camps. Hard upon the heels of the prospector followed the dram-shop, the gambling-hell, and the dance-hall. Every man carried his "Colt," and looked out for his own life and his "claim." Crime went unpunished or was taken in hand, when it got too rampant, by vigilance committees. In the diggings, shaggy frontiersmen and "pikes" from Missouri mingled with the scum of eastern cities and with broken-down business men and young college graduates seeking their fortune. Surveyors and geologists came of necessity, speculators in mining stock and city lots set up their offices in the towns; later came a sprinkling of school-teachers and ministers. Fortunes were made in one day and lost the next at poker or loo. To-day the lucky miner who had struck a good "lead" was drinking champagne out of pails and treating the town; to-morrow he was "busted," and shouldered the pick for a new onslaught upon his luck. This strange, reckless life, was not without fascination, and highly picturesque and dramatic elements were present in it. It was, as Bret Harte says, "an era replete with a certain heroic Greek poetry," and sooner or later it was sure to find its poet. During the war California remained loyal to the Union, but was too far from the seat of conflict to experience any serious disturbance, and went on independently developing its own resources and becoming daily more civilized. By 1868 San Francisco had a literary magazine, the *Overland Monthly*, which ran until 1875. It had a decided local flavor, and the vignette on its title-page was a happily chosen emblem, representing a grizzly bear crossing a railway track. In an early number of the *Overland* was a story entitled the *Luck of Roaring Camp*, by Francis Bret Harte, a native of Albany, N. Y., 1835, who had come to California at the age of seventeen, in time to catch the unique aspects of the life of the Forty-niners, before their vagabond communities had settled down into the law-abiding society of the present day. His first contribution was followed by other stories and sketches of a similar kind, such as the *Outcasts of Poker Flat*, *Miggles*, and *Tennessee's Partner*, and by verses, serious and humorous, of which last, *Plain Language from Truthful James*, better known as the *Heathen Chinee*, made an immediate hit, and carried its author's name into every corner of the English-speaking world. In 1871 he published a collection of his tales, another of his poems, and a volume of very clever parodies, *Condensed Novels*, which rank with Thackeray's *Novels by Eminent Hands*. Bret Harte's California stories were vivid, highly-colored pictures of life in the mining camps and raw towns of the Pacific coast. The pathetic and the grotesque went hand in hand in them, and the author aimed to show how even in the desperate characters gathered together there—the fortune hunters, gamblers, thieves, murderers, drunkards, and prostitutes—the latent nobility of human nature asserted itself in acts of heroism, magnanimity, self-sacrifice, and touching fidelity. The same men who cheated at cards and shot each another down with tipsy curses were capable on occasion of the most romantic generosity and the most delicate chivalry. Critics were not wanting who held that, in the matter of dialect and manners and other details, the narrator was not true to the facts. This was a comparatively unimportant charge; but a more serious question was the doubt whether his characters were essentially true to human nature, whether the wild soil of revenge and greed and dissolute living ever yields such flowers of devotion as blossom in *Tennessee's Partner* and the *Outcasts of Poker Flat*. However this may be, there is no question as to Harte's power as a narrator. His short stories are skillfully constructed and effectively told. They never drag, and are never overladen with description, reflection, or other lumber.

In his poems in dialect we find the same variety of types and nationalities characteristic of the Pacific coast: the little Mexican maiden, Pachita, in the old mission garden; the wicked Bill Nye, who tries to cheat the Heathen Chinee at euchre and to rob Injin Dick of his winning lottery ticket; the geological society on the Stanislaw who settle their scientific debates with chunks of old red sandstone and the skulls of mammoths; the unlucky Mr. Dow, who finally strikes gold while digging a well, and builds a house with a "coopilow;" and Flynn, of Virginia, who saves his " pard's " life, at the sacrifice of his own, by holding up the timbers in the caving tunnel. These poems are mostly in monologue, like Browning's dramatic lyrics, exclamatory and abrupt in style, and with a good deal of indicated action, as in *Jim*, where a miner comes into a bar-room, looking for his old chum, learns that he is dead, and is just turning away to hide his emotion, when he recognizes Jim in his informant:

> " Well, thar—Good-by—
> No more, sir—I—
> Eh ?
> What's that you say ?—
> Why, dern it!—sho!—
> No? Yes! By Jo!
> Sold!
> Sold! Why, you limb;
> You ornery,
> Derned old
> Long-legged Jim!"

Bret Harte had many imitators, and not only did our newspaper poetry for a number of years abound in the properties of Californian life, such as gulches, placers, divides, etc., but writers further east applied his method to other conditions. Of these by far the most successful was John Hay, a native of Indiana and private secretary to President Lincoln, whose *Little Breeches*, *Jim Bludso*, and *Mystery of Gilgal* have rivaled Bret Harte's own verses in popularity. In the last-named piece the reader is given to feel that there is something rather cheerful and humorous in a bar-room fight which results in "the gals that winter, as a rule," going " alone to the singing school." In the two former we have heroes of the Bret Harte type, the same combination of superficial wickedness with inherent loyalty and tenderness. The profane farmer of the South-west, who "doesn't pan out on the prophets," and who had taught his little son " to chaw terbacker, just to keep his milk-teeth white," but who believes in God and the angels ever since the miraculous recovery of the same little son when lost on the prairie in a blizzard; and the unsaintly and bigamistic captain of the *Prairie Belle*, who died like a hero, holding the nozzle of his burning boat against the bank

" Till the last galoot's ashore."

The manners and dialect of other classes and sections of the country have received abundant illustration of late years. Edward Eggleston's *Hoosier Schoolmaster*, 1871, and his other novels are pictures of rural life in the early days of Indiana. *Western Windows*, a volume of poems by John James Piatt, another native of Indiana, had an unmistakable local coloring. Charles G. Leland, of Philadelphia, in his *Hans Breitmann* ballads, in dialect, gave a humorous presentation of the German-American element in the cities. By the death, in 1881, of Sidney Lanier, a Georgian by birth, the South lost a poet of rare promise, whose original genius was somewhat hampered by his hesitation between two arts of expression, music and verse, and by his effort to co-ordinate them. His *Science of English Verse*, 1880, was a most suggestive, though hardly convincing, statement of that theory of their relation which he was working out in his practice. Some of his pieces, like the *Mocking Bird* and the *Song of the Chatta-hoochie*, are the most characteristically Southern poetry that has been written in America. Joel Chandler Harris's *Uncle Remus* stories, in Negro dialect, are transcripts from the folk-lore of the plantations, while his collection of stories, *At Teague Poteet's*, together with Miss Murfree's *In the Tennessee Mountains* and her other books have made the Northern public familiar with the wild life of the "moonshiners," who distill illicit whiskey in the mountains of Georgia, North Carolina, and Tennessee. These tales are not only exciting in incident, but strong and fresh in their delineations of character. Their descriptions of mountain scenery are also impressive, though, in the case of the last named writer, frequently too prolonged. George W. Cable's sketches of French Creole life in New Orleans attracted attention by their freshness and quaintness when published in the magazines and re-issued in book form as *Old Creole Days*, in 1879. His first regular novel, the *Grandissimes*, 1880, was likewise a story of Creole life. It had the same winning qualities as his short stories and sketches, but was an advance upon them in dramatic force, especially in the intensely tragic and powerfully told episode of "Bras Coupé." Mr. Cable has continued his studies of Louisiana types and ways in his later books, but the *Grandissimes* still remains his master-piece. All in all, he is, thus far, the most important literary figure of the New South, and the justness and delicacy of his representations of life speak volumes for the sobering and refining agency of the civil war in the States whose "cause" was "lost," but whose true interests gained even more by the loss than did the interests of the victorious North.

The four writers last mentioned have all come to the front within the past eight or ten years, and, in accordance with the plan of this sketch, receive here a mere passing notice. It remains to close our review of the literary history of the period since the war with a somewhat more extended account of the two favorite novelists whose work has done more than any thing else to shape the movement of recent fiction. These are Henry James, Jr., and William Dean Howells. Their writings, though dissimilar in some respects, are alike in this, that they are analytic in method and realistic in spirit. Cooper was a romancer pure and simple; he wrote the romance of adventure and of external incident. Hawthorne went much deeper, and with a finer spiritual insight dealt with the real passions of the heart and with men's inner experiences. This he did with truth and power; but, although himself a keen observer of whatever passed before his eyes, he was not careful to secure a photographic fidelity to the surface facts of speech, dress, manners, etc. Thus the talk of his characters is book talk, and not the actual language of the parlor or the street, with its slang, its colloquial ease and the intonations and shadings of phrase and pronunciation which mark different sections of the country and different grades of society. His attempts at dialect, for example, were of the slenderest kind. His art is ideal, and his romances certainly do not rank as novels of real life. But with the growth of a richer and more complicated society in America fiction has grown more social and more minute in its observation. It would not be fair to classify the novels of James and Howells as the fiction of manners merely; they are also the fiction of character, but they aim to describe people not only as they are, in their inmost natures, but also as they look and talk and dress. They try to express character through manners, which is the way in which it is most often expressed in the daily existence of a conventional society. It is a principle of realism not to select exceptional persons or occurrences, but to take average men and women and their average experiences. The realists protest that the moving incident is not their trade, and that the stories have all been told. They want no plot and no hero. They will tell no rounded tale with a *dénouement*, in which all the parts are distributed, as in the fifth act of an old-fashioned comedy; but they will take a transcript from life and end when they get through, without informing the reader what becomes of the characters. And they will try to interest this reader in "poor real life" with its "foolish face." Their acknowledged masters are Balzac, George Eliot, Turgénieff, and Anthony

Trollope, and they regard novels as studies in sociology, honest reports of the writer's impressions, which may not be without a certain scientific value even.

Mr. James's peculiar province is the international novel; a field which he created for himself, but which he has occupied in company with Howells, Mrs. Burnett, and many others. He was born into the best traditions of New England culture, his father being a resident of Cambridge, and a forcible writer on philosophical subjects, and his brother, William James, a professor in Harvard University. The novelist received most of his schooling in Europe, and has lived much abroad, with the result that he has become half denationalized and has engrafted a cosmopolitan indifference upon his Yankee inheritance. This, indeed, has constituted his opportunity. A close observer and a conscientious student of the literary art, he has added to his intellectual equipment the advantage of a curious doubleness in his point of view. He looks at America with the eyes of a foreigner and at Europe with the eyes of an American. He has so far thrown himself out of relation with American life that he describes a Boston horse-car or a New York hotel table with a sort of amused wonder. His starting-point was in criticism, and he has always maintained the critical attitude. He took up story-writing in order to help himself, by practical experiment, in his chosen art of literary criticism, and his volume on

French Poets and Novelists, 1878, is by no means the least valuable of his books. His short stories in the magazines were collected into a volume in 1875, with the title, *A Passionate Pilgrim and Other Stories*. One or two of these, as the *Last of the Valerii* and the *Madonna of the Future*, suggest Hawthorne, a very unsympathetic study of whom James afterward contributed to the "English Men of Letters" series. But in the name-story of the collection he was already in the line of his future development. This is the story of a middle-aged invalid American, who comes to England in search of health, and finds, too late, in the mellow atmosphere of the mother country, the repose and the congenial surroundings which he has all his life been longing for in his raw America. The pathos of his self-analysis and his confession of failure is subtly imagined. The impressions which he and his far-away English kinsfolk make on one another, their mutual attraction and repulsion, are described with that delicate perception of national differences which makes the humor and sometimes the tragedy of James's later books, like the *American*, *Daisy Miller*, the *Europeans*, and *An International Episode*. His first novel was *Roderick Hudson*, 1876, not the most characteristic of his fictions, but perhaps the most powerful in its grasp of elementary passion. The analytic method and the critical attitude have their dangers in imaginative literature. In proportion as this writer's faculty of minute observation and his realistic objectivity have increased upon him, the uncomfortable coldness which is felt in his youthful work has become actually disagreeable, and his art—growing constantly finer and surer in matters of detail—has seemed to dwell more and more in the region of mere manners and less in the higher realm of character and passion. In most of his writings the heart, somehow, is left out. We have seen that Irving, from his knowledge of England and America, and his long residence in both countries, became the mediator between the two great branches of the Anglo-Saxon race. This he did by the power of his sympathy with each. Henry James has likewise interpreted the two nations to one another in a subtler but less genial fashion than Irving, and not through sympathy, but through contrast, by bringing into relief the opposing ideals of life and society which have developed under different institutions. In his novel, the *American*, 1877, he has shown the actual misery which may result from the clashing of opposed social systems. In such clever sketches as *Daisy Miller*, 1879, the *Pension Beaurepas*, and *A Bundle of Letters*, he has exhibited types of the American girl, the American business man, the æsthetic feebling from Boston, and the Europeanized or would-be denationalized American campaigners in the Old World, and has set forth the ludicrous incongruities, perplexities, and misunderstandings which result from contradictory standards of conventional morality and behavior. In the *Europeans*, 1879, and an *Inter-*

national Episode, 1878, he has reversed the process, bringing Old World standards to the test of American ideas by transferring his *dramatis personæ* to republican soil. The last-named of these illustrates how slender a plot realism requires for its purposes. It is nothing more than the history of an English girl of good family who marries an American gentleman and undertakes to live in America, but finds herself so uncomfortable in strange social conditions that she returns to England for life, while, contrariwise, the heroine's sister is so taken with the freedom of these very conditions that she elopes with another American and "goes West." James is a keen observer of the physiognomy of cities as well as of men, and his *Portraits of Places*, 1884, is among the most delightful contributions to the literature of foreign travel.

Mr. Howells's writings are not without "international" touches. In *A Foregone Conclusion* and the *Lady of the Aroostook*, and others of his novels, the contrasted points of view in American and European life are introduced, and especially those variations in feeling, custom, dialect, etc., which make the modern Englishman and the modern American such objects of curiosity to each other, and which have been dwelt upon of late even unto satiety. But in general he finds his subjects at home, and if he does not know his own countrymen and countrywomen more intimately than Mr. James, at least

LITERATURE SINCE 1861. 275

he loves them better. There is a warmer sentiment in his fictions, too; his men are better fellows and his women are more lovable. Howells was born in Ohio. His early life was that of a western country editor. In 1860 he published, jointly with his friend Piatt, a book of verse— *Poems of Two Friends*. In 1861 he was sent as consul to Venice, and the literary results of his sojourn there appeared in his sketches *Venetian Life*, 1865, and *Italian Journeys*, 1867. In 1871 he became editor of the *Atlantic Monthly*, and in the same year published his *Suburban Sketches*. All of these early volumes showed a quick eye for the picturesque, an unusual power of description, and humor of the most delicate quality; but as yet there was little approach to narrative. *Their Wedding Journey* was a revelation to the public of the interest that may lie in an ordinary bridal trip across the State of New York, when a close and sympathetic observation is brought to bear upon the characteristics of American life as it appears at railway stations and hotels, on steam-boats and in the streets of very commonplace towns. *A Chance Acquaintance*, 1873, was Howells's first novel, though even yet the story was set against a background of travel—pictures, a holiday trip on the St. Lawrence and the Saguenay; and descriptions of Quebec and the Falls of Montmorenci, etc., rather predominated over the narrative. Thus, gradually and by a natural process, complete characters and realistic novels, such as *A Modern In-*

stance, 1882, and *Indian Summer*, evolved themselves from truthful sketches of places and persons seen by the way.

The incompatibility existing between European and American views of life, which makes the comedy or the tragedy of Henry James's international fictions, is replaced in Howells's novels by the repulsion between differing social grades in the same country. The adjustment of these subtle distinctions forms a part of the problem of life in all complicated societies. Thus in *A Chance Acquaintance* the heroine is a bright and pretty Western girl, who becomes engaged during a pleasure tour to an irreproachable but offensively priggish young gentleman from Boston, and the engagement is broken by her in consequence of an unintended slight—the betrayal on the hero's part of a shade of mortification when he and his betrothed are suddenly brought into the presence of some fashionable ladies belonging to his own *monde*. The little comedy, *Out of the Question*, deals with this same adjustment of social scales; and in many of Howells's other novels, such as *Silas Lapham* and the *Lady of the Aroostook*, one of the main motives may be described to be the contact of the man who eats with his fork with the man who eats with his knife, and the shock thereby ensuing. In *Indian Summer* the complications arise from the difference in age between the hero and heroine, and not from a difference in station or social antecedents. In all of these fictions the misunderstandings come from an incompatibility of manners rather than of character, and, if any thing were to be objected to the probability of the story, it is that the climax hinges on delicacies and subtleties which, in real life, when there is opportunity for explanations, are readily brushed aside. But in *A Modern Instance* Howells touched the deeper springs of action. In this, his strongest work, the catastrophe is brought about, as in George Eliot's great novels, by the reaction of characters upon one another, and the story is realistic in a higher sense than any mere study of manners can be. His nearest approach to romance is in the *Undiscovered Country*, 1880, which deals with the Spiritualists and the Shakers, and in its study of problems that hover on the borders of the supernatural, in its out-of-the-way personages and adventures, and in a certain ideal poetic flavor about the whole book, has a strong resemblance to Hawthorne, especially to Hawthorne in the *Blithedale Romance*, where he comes closer to common ground with other romancers. It is interesting to compare the *Undiscovered Country* with Henry James's *Bostonians*, the latest and one of the cleverest of his fictions, which is likewise a study of the clairvoyants, mediums, woman's rights' advocates, and all varieties of cranks, reformers, and patrons of "causes," for whom Boston has long been notorious. A most unlovely race of people they become under the cold scrutiny of Mr. James's cosmopolitan eyes, which see more clearly the charlatanism, narrow-mindedness, mistaken fanaticism, morbid self-consciousness, disagreeable nervous intensity, and vulgar or ridiculous outside peculiarities of the humanitarians, than the nobility and moral enthusiasm which underlie the surface.

Howells is almost the only successful American dramatist, and this in the field of parlor comedy. His little farces, the *Elevator*, the *Register*, the *Parlor Car*, etc., have a lightness and grace, with an exquisitely absurd situation, which remind us more of the *Comedies et Proverbes* of Alfred de Musset, or the many agreeable dialogues and monologues of the French domestic stage, than of any work of English or American hands. His softly ironical yet affectionate treatment of feminine ways is especially admirable. In his numerous types of sweetly illogical, inconsistent, and inconsequent womanhood he has perpetuated with a nicer art than Dickens what Thackeray calls "that great discovery," Mrs. Nickleby.

1. Theodore Winthrop. Life in the Open Air. Cecil Dreeme.
2. Thomas Wentworth Higginson. Life in a Black Regiment.
3. Poetry of the Civil War. Edited by Richard Grant White. New York: 1866.
4. Charles Farrar Browne. Artemus Ward — His Book. Lecture on the Mormons. Artemus Ward in London.

5. Samuel Langhorne Clemens. The Jumping Frog. Roughing It. The Mississippi Pilot.
6. Charles Godfrey Leland. Hans Breitmann's Ballads.
7. Edward Everett Hale. If, Yes, and Perhaps. His Level Best and Other Stories.
8. Francis Bret Harte. Outcasts of Poker Flat and Other Stories. Condensed Novels. Poems in Dialect.
9. Sidney Lanier. Nirvâna. Resurrection. The Harlequin of Dreams. Song of the Chattahoochie. The Mocking Bird. The Stirrup-Cup. Tampa Robins. The Bee. The Revenge of Hamish. The Ship of Earth. The Marshes of Glynn. Sunrise.
10. Henry James, Jr. A Passionate Pilgrim. Roderick Hudson. Daisy Miller. Pension Beaurepas. A Bundle of Letters. An International Episode. The Bostonians. Portraits of Places.
11. William Dean Howells. Their Wedding Journey. Suburban Sketches. A Chance Acquaintance. A Foregone Conclusion. The Undiscovered Country A Modern Instance.
12. George W. Cable. Old Creole Days. Madam Delphine. The Grandissimes.
13. Joel Chandler Harris. Uncle Remus. Mingo and Other Sketches.
14. Charles Egbert Craddock (Miss Murfree). In the Tennessee Mountains.

INDEX.

An Index to the American Authors and Writings, and the Principal American Periodicals mentioned in this Volume.

Abraham Lincoln, 188.
Adams and Liberty, 74.
Adams, J. Q., 92, 109.
Adams, Samuel, 52–54.
After-Dinner Poem, 177.
After the Funeral, 187.
Age of Reason, the, 64–66, 75.
Ages, the, 201.
Alcott, A. B., 135, 136.
Aldrich T. B., 260.
Algerine Captive, the, 79.
Algic Researches, 171.
Alhambra, the, 94.
All Quiet Along the Potomac, 242.
Alnwick Castle, 103.
Æsop, Richard, 68, 69.
American, the, 272, 273.
American Civil War, the, 241.
American Conflict, the, 241.
American Flag, the, 102.
American Note-Books, 123, 149, 151, 155, 168.
American Scholar, the, 120, 135, 160.
Ames, Fisher, 62, 63.
Among My Books, 188.
Anarchiad, the, 69.
Annabel Lee, 217.
Army Life in a Black Regiment, 245.
Army of the Potomac, the, 241.
Art of Book Making, the, 99.
"Artemus Ward," 248, 251–56.
Arthur Mervyn, 80.
At Teague Poteet's, 268.
Atlantic Monthly, the, 178, 187, 197–199, 244, 245, 257, 261, 275.
Atlantis, 222.
Auf Wiederschen, 187.
Autobiography, Franklin's, 33, 46, 48, 49.
Autocrat of the Breakfast Table, the, 173, 179.

Backwoodsman, the, 91.
Ballad of the Oysterman, 174.
Bancroft, George, 161, 181, 190, 191.
Barbara Frietchie, 207.
Barlow, Joel, 68–71.
Battle Hymn of the Republic, 242.
Battle of the Kegs, 74.
Battlefield, the, 203.
Bay Fight, the, 243.
Bay Psalm Book, the, 23.
Bedouin Song, 226.
Beecher, Lyman, 127, 231.
Beecher, H. W., 231.
Beers, Mrs. E. L., 242.
Beleaguered City, the, 165, 169.
Belfry of Bruges, the, 165, 167.
Berkeley, Robert, 18.
Biglow Papers, the, 182, 183, 185, 186, 209, 248.
Black Cat, the, 218.
Black Fox of Salmon River, the, 206.
Blair, Jas., 13.
Blithedale Romance, the, 123, 154, 227, 277.
Bloody Tenet of Persecution, the, 25.
Blue and the Gray, the, 243.
Boker, G. H., 260.
Bostonians, the, 277.
Bracebridge Hall, 96, 98, 247.
Bradford's Journal, 24, 28.
Brahma, 136, 141.
Brainard, J. G. C., 205, 206, 230.
Brick Moon, the, 259.
Bridal of Pennacook, the, 206, 209.
Bridge, the, 167, 168.
Broken Heart, the, 99.
Brown, C. B., 79–82.
Browne, C. F., 250, 251.
Brownell, H. H., 242–44.
Bryant, W. C., 86, 102, 163, 199–204.
Buccaneer, the, 115.

Building of the Ship, the, 167.
Bundle of Letters, A, 273.
Burnett, Mrs. F. H., 271.
Bushnell, Horace, 128.
Busy-Body, the, 45, 66.
Butler, W. A., 224.
Byrd, Wm., 17.

Cable, G. W., 268.
Calhoun, J. C., 56, 110, 111.
Cambridge Thirty Years Ago, 161.
Cape Cod, 144.
Capture of Fugitive Slaves, 184.
Cary, Alice, 228.
Cary, Phoebe, 228.
Cask of Amontillado, the, 218.
Cassandra Southwick, 209.
Cathedral, the, 189.
Cecil Dreeme, 245.
Century Magazine, the, 197, 241, 261.
Chambered Nautilus, the, 176.
Chance Acquaintance, A, 275, 276.
Channing, W. E., 115-18, 120, 126, 130, 138.
Channing, W. E., Jr., 138, 156.
Channing, W. H., 138.
Chapel of the Hermits, the, 208.
Character of Milton, the, 117.
Charleston, 243.
Children of Adam, 233.
Choate, Rufus, 114, 115.
Christian Examiner, the, 117.
Circular Letter, by Otis & Quincy, 55.
City in the Sea, the, 214.
Clara Howard, 80.
Clarke, J. F., 138.
Clay, Henry, 110, 111.
Clemens, S. L., 250, 255-57.
Columbiad, the, 70, 71.
Common Sense, 63.
Condensed Novels, 264.
Conduct of Life, the, 139.
Confederate States of America, the, 241.
Conquest of Canaan, 72, 100.
Conquest of Granada, 94.
Conquest of Mexico, 190.
Conquest of Peru, 190.
Conspiracy of Pontiac, the, 192.
Constitution and the Union, the, 112.
Constitution of the United States, the, 55, 59.
Contentment, 109.
Contrast, the, 79.
Conversations on the Gospels, 135.
Conversations on Some of the Old Poets, 187.
Cooke, J. E., 222.

Cooper, J. F., 77, 91, 104-8, 114, 171, 269.
Coral Grove, the, 230.
Cotton, John, 25, 32.
Count Frontenac & New France, 193.
Courtin', the, 185, 248.
Courtship of Miles Standish, the, 30.
Cow Chase, the, 73.
Cranch, C. P., 123, 138.
Crisis, the, 63.
Croaker Papers, the, 103.
Culprit Fay, the, 102.
Curtis, G. W., 123, 260.

Daisy Miller, 272, 273.
Dana, C. A., 122, 138, 199.
Dana, R. H., 86, 115.
Danbury News Man, 74, 250.
Dante, Longfellow's, 172.
Davis, Jefferson, 241.
Day of Doom, the, 40.
Death of the Flowers, the, 201, 202.
Declaration of Independence, the, 55.
Deerslayer, the, 106, 108.
Democratic Vistas, 236.
Derby, G. H., 250.
Descent into the Maelstrom, 219.
Deserted Road, the, 228.
Dial, the, 120, 127, 136, 138.
Dialogue Between Franklin and the Gout, 48.
Diamond Lens, the, 245.
Discourse of the Plantation of Virginia, A, 11.
Dolph Heyliger, 96.
Domain of Arnheim, the, 219.
Dorchester Giant, the, 173.
Drake, J. R., 102, 103, 115.
Draper, J. W., 241.
Dream Life, 231.
Dresser, the Wound, 235.
Drifting, 228.
Driving Home the Cows, 242.
Drum Taps, 236.
Dutchman's Fireside, the, 102.
Dwight, J. S., 123, 130, 138.
Dwight, Theodore, 68, 69.
Dwight, Timothy, 68, 72.

Early Spring in Massachusetts, 144.
Echo, the, 69.
Echo Club, the, 226.
Edgar Huntley, 80.
Edith Linsey, 223.
Edwards, Jonathan, 41-44, 72, 126, 128.
Eggleston, Edward, 267.
Elevator, the, 278.

Eliot, John, 23.
Elsie Venner, 180.
Emerson, R. W., 113, 120, 121, 125, 147, 156, 160, 169, 208, 235.
Endicott's Red Cross, 153.
English Note Books, 155.
English Traits, 134, 142.
Ephemeræ, 231.
Epilogue to Cato, 76.
Eternal Goodness, 208.
Ethan Brand, 152.
Evangeline, 169, 170.
Evening Wind, the, 201.
Everett, Edward, 114, 115, 181.
Europeans, the, 272, 273.
Excelsior, 166.
Excursions, 144.
Expediency of the Federal Constitution, 59.
Eyes and Ears, 231.

F. Smith, 223.
Fable for Critics, A, 137, 187, 189.
Facts in the Case of M. Valdemar, the, 215.
Fall of the House of Usher, the, 218.
Familists' Hymn, the, 29.
Fanshawe, 151.
Farewell Address, Washington's, 60.
Faust, Taylor's, 226.
Federalist, the, 60.
Ferdinand and Isabella, 161, 190.
Final Judgment, the, 42.
Finch, F. M., 243.
Fire of Driftwood, the, 167.
Fireside Travels, 161.
Fitz Adam's Story, 185.
Flint, Timothy, 91.
Flood of Years, the, 203.
Footpath, the, 187.
Footsteps of Angels, 165.
Foregone Conclusion, A, 274.
Forest Hymn, 200.
Fortune of the Republic, 139, 140.
Foster, S. C., 228, 229.
France and England in North America, 192.
Franklin, Ben., 33, 44-49, 66.
Freedom of the Will, 42.
French Poets and Novelists, 272.
Freneau, Philip, 76, 77.
Fuller, Margaret, 121-23, 128, 130, 135-38, 142, 156, 171.

Galaxy Magazine, the, 261.
Garrison, W. L., 110, 112, 193, 205, 229.
Garrison of Cape Ann, the, 38.
General History of Virginia, 15.

Geography of the Mississippi Valley, 91.
Georgia Spec, the, 79.
Ghost Ball at Congress Hall, the, 223.
Give Me the Old. 224.
Godey's Lady's Book, 197, 210.
Godfrey, Thos., 79.
Gold Bug, the, 215.
Golden Legend, the, 171.
Good News from Virginia, 19.
Good Word for Winter, A, 188.
Goodrich, S. G., 88, 92, 151.
Grandfather's Chair, 38.
Grandissimes, the, 268.
Greeley, Horace, 123, 225.
Green River, 201.
Greene, A. G., 109.
Greenfield Hill, 72.
Guardian Angel, the, 180.

Hail, Columbia! 74.
Hale, E. E., 160, 215, 257-60.
Halleck, F. G., 103, 104, 115.
Halpine, C. G., 245.
Hamilton, Alexander, 59-61, 63, 112.
Hannah Thurston, 227.
Hans Breitmann Ballads, 267.
Hans Pfaall, 215.
Harbinger, the, 122, 123.
Harper's Monthly Magazine, 197, 198, 260, 261.
Harris, J. C., 268.
Harte, F. B., 255, 261, 263-66.
Hasty Pudding, 71.
Haunted Palace, the, 217.
Hawthorne, Julian, 154.
Hawthorne, Nathaniel, 7, 29, 38, 70, 123, 137, 149-156, 168, 181, 227, 240, 247, 248, 269, 272, 277.
Hay, John, 266.
Health, A, 109.
Heathen Chinee, the, 264.
Hedge, F. H., 123.
Height of the Ridiculous, the, 173.
Henry, Patrick, 52-54, 59.
Hiawatha, 77, 170.
Higginson, T. W., 95, 123, 137, 245.
His Level Best, 258.
History of the Dividing Line, 17.
History of New England, Winthrop's, 28-32.
History of Plymouth Plantation, Bradford's, 28.
History of the United Netherlands, 191.
History of the United States, Bancroft's, 161, 191: Higginson's, 95.

American Literature—Index. 283

History of Virginia, Berkeley's, 18: Stith's, 18.
Hoffman, C. F., 224.
Holland, J. G., 261.
Holmes, O. W., 109, 160, 161, 172-181, 202, 245, 247, 248.
Home, Sweet Home, 108.
Homesick in Heaven, 176.
Hooker, Thos., 32, 35, 128.
Hoosier Schoolmaster, the, 267.
Hopkins, Lemuel, 68, 69.
Hopkinson, Francis, 74.
Hopkinson, Joseph, 74.
Horse-Shoe Robinson, 221.
House of the Seven Gables, the, 150, 154.
Howe, Mrs. J. W., 242.
Howells, W. D., 269-271, 274-78.
Humphreys, David, 68, 69.
Hymn at the Completion of Concord Monument, 143.
Hymn of the Moravian Nuns, 163.
Hymn to the Night, 165.
Hymn to the North Star, 200.
Hyperion, 172.

Ichabod, 207.
If, Yes, and Perhaps, 258.
Iliad, Bryant's, 204.
Illustrious Providences, 34.
In the Tennessee Mountains, 268.
In the Twilight, 187.
In War Time, 207.
Independent, the, 231.
Indian Bible, Eliot's, 23.
Indian Burying Ground, the, 76, 77.
Indian Student, the, 76.
Indian Summer, 276.
Ingham Papers, 258.
Inklings of Adventure, 223.
Innocents Abroad, 255, 256.
International Episode, An, 272, 273.
Irving, Washington, 86, 91, 92, 93-101, 201, 247, 248, 257 273.
Israfel, 214.
Italian Journeys, 275.
Italian Note-Books, 155.

James, Henry, 245, 269-74, 276, 277.
Jane Talbot, 80.
Jay, John, 60, 61.
Jefferson, Thos., 14, 55-59, 62.
Jesuits in North America, the, 193.
Jim, 265.
Jim Bludso, 266.
John Brown's Body, 73, 242.
John Godfrey's Fortune, 227.
John Phœnix, 250.

John Underhill, 29.
Jonathan to John, 185.
"Josh Billings," 255.
Journey to the Land of Eden, A, 17.
Judd, Sylvester, 189.
Jumping Frog, the, 255.
June, 201, 202.
Justice and Expediency, 206.

Kansas and Nebraska Bill, the, 195.
Katie, 243.
Kennedy, J. P., 221.
Key, F. S., 75.
Kidd, the Pirate, 96.
King's Missive, the, 209.
Knickerbocker Magazine, the, 96, 101, 151, 192, 210.
Knickerbocker's History of New York, 86, 96, 97, 247.

Lady of the Aroostook, the, 274, 276.
Lanier, Sidney, 267.
La Salle and the Discovery of the Great West, 193.
Last Leaf, the, 109, 174.
Last of the Mohicans, the, 106, 108.
Last of the Valerii, the, 272.
Latest Form of Infidelity, the, 128.
Laus Deo, 207.
Leatherstocking Tales, 77, 106, 107.
Leaves of Grass, 232, 233, 236.
Lecture on the Mormons, 252.
Legend of Brittany, 182.
Legend of Sleepy Hollow, 96, 98.
Legends of New England, 206.
Legends of the Province House, 153.
Leland, C. G., 267.
Letter on Whitewashing, 74.
Letters and Social Aims, 139.
Letters from Under a Bridge, 223.
Letters of a Traveler, 204.
Liberator, the, 110, 193, 229.
Life of Columbus, 94, 100.
Life of Goldsmith, 100.
Life of John of Barneveld, 192.
Life of Washington, 100.
Ligeia, 218.
Light of Stars, the, 165.
Lincoln, Abraham, 188, 245-47, 249.
Lines on Leaving Europe, 223.
Lippincott's Magazine, 261.
Literary Recreations, 210.
Literati of New York, 211.
Little Breeches, 265.
Livingston, Wm., 66.
Longfellow, H. W., 29, 77, 149, 160-172, 183, 198, 231.
Lost Arts, 194.

284   AMERICAN LITERATURE—INDEX.

Lost Cause, the, 241.
Lowell, J. R., 124, 135, 137, 139, 160, 161, 168, 181-189, 199, 202, 247, 248
Luck of Roaring Camp, the, 263.
Lunatic's Skate, the, 223.
Lyrics of a Day, 243.

MacFingal, 67, 68, 74.
Madonna of the Future, the, 272.
Magnalia, Christi Americana, 20, 33-36, 40.
Mahomet and his Successors, 100.
Maine Woods, the, 144.
"Major Jack Downing," 250.
Man of the Crowd, the, 218.
Man-of-War Bird, the, 236.
Man Without a Country, the, 215, 257.
Marble Faun, the, 150, 152, 154, 155.
Marco Bozzaris, 103.
Margaret, 189.
Mark Twain, 248, 255-57.
Maryland, My Maryland, 242.
Masque of the Gods, the, 225.
Masque of the Red Death, 218.
Mather, Cotton, 20, 23, 24, 26, 30, 33-38, 40.
Mather, Increase, 34.
Maud Muller, 208.
May Day, 139.
Maypole of Merrymount, the, 29.
Memoranda of the Civil War, 236.
Memorial History of Boston, 209.
Men Naturally God's Enemies, 42.
Merry Mount, 190.
Messenger, R. H., 224.
Miggles, 264.
"Miles O'Reilly," 245.
Minister's Black Veil, the, 153.
Minister's Wooing, the, 230.
Mitchell, D. G., 230, 231.
Mocking Bird, the, 268.
Modern Instance, A, 275, 277.
Modern Learning, 74.
Modest Request, A, 175.
Money Diggers, the, 96.
Montcalm and Wolfe, 193.
Monterey, 224.
Moore, C. C., 224.
Moore, Frank, 241.
Moral Argument Against Calvinism, the, 117.
Morris, G. P., 223.
Morton's Hope, 190.
Mosses from an Old Manse, 149, 153.
Motley, J. L., 160, 190-92.
Mount Vernon, 70.
"Mrs. Partington," 250.

MS. Found in a Bottle, 221.
Murder of Lovejoy, the, 160.
Murders in the Rue Morgue, the, 215.
Music Grinders, the, 174.
My Aunt, 174.
My Captain, 237.
My Double and How He Undid Me, 259.
My Garden Acquaintance, 188.
My Life is Like the Summer Rose, 108.
My Study Windows, 188.
My Wife and I, 230.
Mystery of Gilgal, the, 266.
Mystery of Marie Roget, the, 215.

Narrative of A. Gordon Pym, the, 219.
Nathaniel Hawthorne and His Wife, 154.
Nature, 120, 131, 134.
Naval History of the United States, 104.
Nearer Home, 228.
Negro Melodies, 228.
New England Tragedies, 29.
New England Two Centuries Ago, 188.
New System of English Grammar, A, 250.
New York Evening Post, the, 200, 204.
New York Tribune, the, 122, 136.
Newell, R. H., 255.
North American Review, the, 114, 115, 151, 162, 187, 199, 200.
Norton, Andrews, 128.
Notes on Virginia, 58.
Nothing to Wear, 224.
Nux Postcœnatica, 175.
Nye, Bill, 255.

O'Brien, F. J., 245.
Observations on the Boston Port Bill, 55.
Occulation of Orion, the, 167, 183.
Ode at the Harvard Commemoration, 187.
Ode for a Social Meeting, 175.
Ode to Freedom, 184.
Odyssey, Bryant's, 204.
Old Clock on the Stairs, the, 167.
Old Creole Days, 268.
Old Grimes, 109.
Old Ironsides, 173.
Old Oaken Bucket, the, 108.
Old Pennsylvania Farmer, the, 225.
Old Régime in Canada, the, 193.

Old Sergeant, the, 242.
On a Certain Condescension in Foreigners, 185.
One Hoss Shay, the, 176, 248.
Oregon Trail, the, 192.
Ormond, 80, 81.
"Orpheus C. Kerr," 255.
Orphic Sayings, 136.
Osgood, Mrs. K. P., 242.
Otis, James, 52-55.
Our Master, 208.
Our Old Home, 155.
Out of the Question, 276.
Outcasts of Poker Flat, the, 264, 265.
Outre Mer, 163.
Overland Monthly, the, 263.
Over-Soul, the, 136.

Paine, R. T., 75.
Paine, Tom, 63, 66.
Panorama, the, 207.
Paper, 48.
Parker, Theodore, 126, 127, 129, 130, 138.
Parkman, Francis, 161, 190-93.
Parlor Car, the, 278.
Partisan, the, 222.
Passionate Pilgrim, A, 272.
Pathfinder, the, 106.
Paulding, J. K., 91, 95, 101.
Payne, J. H., 108.
Pearl of Orr's Island, the, 230.
Pencillings by the Way, 222.
Pension Beaurepas, the, 273.
Percival, J. G., 230.
Percy, Geo., 11.
"Peter Parley," 88.
"Petroleum V. Nasby," 255.
Phenomena Quædam Apocalyptica, 39.
Phillips, Wendell, 160, 193, 194.
Philosophic Solitude, 66.
Philosophy of Composition, 214.
Phœnixiana, 250.
Piatt, J. J., 242, 267, 275.
Pictures of Memory, 228.
Pilot, the, 107.
Pink and White Tyranny, 230.
Pinkney, E. C., 109.
Pioneer, the, 181.
Pioneers, the, 91, 106.
Pioneers of France in the New World, 193.
Plain Language from Truthful James 264.
Planting of the Apple-Tree, the, 203.
Poe, E. A., 109, 138, 151, 181, 201, 210, 212-221, 228, 240, 259.

Poems of the Orient, 225.
Poems of Two Friends, 275.
Poems on Slavery, 168.
Poet at the Breakfast Table, the, 179.
Poetic Principle, the, 216.
Poetry: A Metrical Essay, 174.
Poet's Hope, A, 138.
Political Green House, the, 69.
Pollard, E. A, 241.
Pons Maximus, 227.
Poor Richard's Almanac, 48.
Portraits of Places, 274.
Prairie, the, 106.
Prentice, G. D., 205. 250.
Prescott, W. H., 161, 190, 192, 240.
Present Crisis, the, 184.
Pride of the Village, the, 79.
Prince Deukalion, 225.
Prince of Parthia, the, 79.
Problem, the, 143.
Professor at the Breakfast Table, the, 179.
Progress to the Mines, A, 17.
Prologue, the, 176.
Prophecy of Samuel Sewall, the, 39.
Prophet, the, 225.
Purloined Letter, the, 215.
Putnam's Monthly, 161, 260.

Quaker Widow, the, 225.
Quincy, Josiah, 52-55.

Rag Man and Rag Woman, the, 259.
Randall, J. R., 242.
Randolph, John, 57.
Raven, the, 214, 215, 217.
Read, T. B., 227, 228.
Reaper and the Flowers, the, 165.
Rebellion Record, the, 241.
Recollections of a Lifetime, 88, 92.
Red Rover, the, 107.
Register, the, 278.
Remarks on Associations, 117.
Remarks on National Literature, 118, 130.
Representative Men, 133, 139, 142.
Resignation, 167.
Reveries of a Bachelor, 230.
Rhœcus, 182.
Rhymes of Travel, 225.
Riding to Vote, 242.
Rights of the British Colonies, 55.
Ripley, George, 122, 129, 130, 138, 199.
Rip Van Winkle, 96.
Rip Van Winkle, M.D., 175.
Rise and Fall of the Confederate States, 241.

286 AMERICAN LITERATURE—INDEX.

Rise and Fall of the Slave Power, 241.
Rise of the Dutch Republic, 191.
Rob of the Bowl, 221.
Roderick Hudson, 272.
Roughing It, 255, 256.

Salmagundi, 94, 101, 203.
Sandys, George, 16.
San Francisco, 261.
Scarlet Letter, the, 29, 152-154.
School Days, 205.
Schoolcraft, H. R., 171.
Science of English Verse, 267.
Scribner's Monthly, 261.
Scripture Poems, 222.
Seaside and Fireside, 165, 167.
Seaweed, 167, 169.
Selling of Joseph, the, 39.
September Gale, the, 174.
Sewall, J. M., 76.
Sewall, Samuel, 38, 39.
Shakspere Ode, 115.
Shaw, H. W., 255.
Shepherd of King Admetus, the, 182.
Sheridan's Ride, 228.
Shillaber, B. P., 250.
Sigourney, Mrs. L. H., 230.
Silas Lapham, 276.
Simms, W. G., 221.
Simple Cobbler of Agawam, the, 21.
Sinners in the Hands of an Angry God, 43.
Skeleton in Armor, the, 166.
Skeleton in the Closet, the, 259.
Sketch Book, the, 95, 96, 98.
Skipper Ireson's Ride, 208.
Sleeper, the, 218.
Smith, Elihu, 68.
Smith, John, 9, 11, 15, 16.
Smith, Seba, 250.
Snow-Bound, 208.
Society and Solitude, 139.
Song of the Chattahoochie, 268.
Song for a Temperance Dinner, 175.
Southern Literary Messenger, the, 210, 212.
Southern Passages and Pictures, 222.
Sparkling and Bright, 224.
Specimens of Foreign Standard Literature, 130.
Specimen Days, 236.
Sphinx, the, 177.
Sprague, Charles, 115.
Spring, 223.
Spy, the, 106.
Squibob Papers, 250.
Star Papers, 231.

Star Spangled Banner, the, 75.
Stedman, E. C., 260.
Stephens, A. H., 241.
Stith, William, 18.
Stoddard, R. H., 260.
Story of Kennett, the, 227.
Stowe, Mrs. H. B., 229, 230.
Strachey, William, 9.
Stuart, Moses, 127.
Sumner, Charles, 160, 162, 168, 186, 193-95.
Supernaturalism in New England, 210.
Swallow Barn, 221.
Sybaris and Other Homes, 258.

Tales of the Glauber Spa, 203.
Tales of the Grotesque and Arabesque, 218.
Tales of a Traveler, 95.
Tales of a Wayside Inn, 209.
Tamerlane, 212.
Tanglewood Tales, 155.
Taylor, Bayard, 224-27.
Telling the Bees, 208.
Ten Times One is Ten, 258.
Tennessee's Partner, 264, 265.
Tent on the Beach, the, 209.
Thanatopsis, 86, 102, 163, 200, 201, 203.
The Boys, 175.
Theology, Dwight's, 72.
Their Wedding Journey, 275.
Thirty Poems, 203.
Thoreau, H. D., 121, 124, 138, 142, 148, 156, 160, 235, 240.
Timrod, Henry, 242, 243.
To Helen, 214.
To M—— from Abroad, 223.
To One in Paradise, 217.
To Seneca Lake, 230.
To a Waterfowl, 201.
Tour on the Prairies, A, 91.
Tramp Abroad, A, 255.
Transcendentalist, the, 130, 132.
Travels, Dwight's, 73.
Treatise Concerning Religious Affections, 43.
True Grandeur of Nations, the, 195.
True Relation, Smith's, 15.
True Repertory of the Wrack of Sir Thomas Gates, 9.
Trumbull, John. 67-69.
Triumph of Infidelity, 72.
Twice Told Tales, 151-53.
Two Rivers, 146.
Tyler, Royal, 79.

American Literature—Index.

Ullalume, 217.
Uncle Remus, 268.
Uncle Tom's Cabin, 229, 230.
Under the Willows, 186.
Undiscovered Country, the, 277.
Unknown Dead, the, 243.
Unseen Spirits, 223.

Valley of Unrest, the, 214.
Vanity Fair, 251.
Vassall Morton, 190.
Venetian Life, 275.
Views Afoot, 225.
Villa Franca, 187.
Village Blacksmith, the, 166.
Virginia Comedians, the, 222.
Vision of Columbus, the, 70.
Vision of Sir Launfal, the, 184.
Visit from St. Nicholas, A, 224.
Voices of Freedom, 267.
Voices of the Night, 163, 165.
Voluntaries, 143.
Von Kempelen's Discovery, 215.

Walden, 144.
Wants of Man, the, 109.
War Lyrics, 243.
Ward, Nathaniel, 21.
Ware, Henry, 128.
Washers of the Shroud, the, 187.
Washington, George, 60, 61, 63.
Washington as a Camp, 244.
Washington Square, 245.
Webster, Daniel, 110, 111-114, 115.
Webster's Spelling Book, 88.
Week on the Concord and Merrimac Rivers, A, 144.
Western Windows, 267.
Westminster Abbey, 99.
Westover MSS., the, 17.

Westward Ho! 91.
What Mr. Robinson Thinks, 183.
Whistle, the, 48.
Whitaker, Alexander, 19.
White R. G., 261.
Whitman, Walt, 232-37.
Whittier, J. G., 29, 38, 39, 168, 181, 204-10, 230, 236, 244.
Wieland, 80, 82.
Wigglesworth, Michael, 40.
Wild Honeysuckle, the, 76.
Wilde, R. H., 108.
William Wilson, 218.
Williams, Roger, 25.
Willis, N. P., 90, 202, 222, 223, 225, 231.
Wilson, Forceythe, 242.
Winter Evening Hymn to My Fire, 186.
Winthrop, John. 10, 24, 26, 28-32.
Winthrop, Theodore, 244.
Witchcraft, 188.
Witch's Daughter, the, 206.
Woman in the Nineteenth Century, 136.
Wonder Book, 155.
Wonders of the Invisible World, 24, 38.
Woods, Leonard, 127.
Woods in Winter, 163.
Woodman, Spare that Tree, 224.
Woodworth, Samuel, 108.
Woolman's Journal, 82-84.
Wrath Upon the Wicked, 42.
Wreck of the Hesperus, the, 166, 169.

Yankee Doodle, 73.
Yankee in Canada, 144.
Year's Life, A, 181.
Yemassee, the, 222.

THE END.

www.ingramcontent.com/pod-product-compliance
Lightning Source LLC
Chambersburg PA
CBHW031339230426
43670CB00006B/387